P9-DDF-364

BEST OF BUGIALLI

THE BEST OF
Bugialli

BY

GIULIANO BUGIALLI

PHOTOGRAPHS BY

JOHN DOMINIS

Stewart, Tabori & Chang

NEW YORK

Published by Stewart, Tabori & Chang, Inc.
575 Broadway, New York, New York 10012

Distributed in Canada by General Publishing Co. Ltd.
30 Lesmill Road, Don Mills, Ontario, Canada M3B 2T6

Distributed in the English language elsewhere in the world (except
Central and South America) by Melia Publishing Services,
P.O. BOX 1639, Maidenhead, Berkshire SL6 6YZ England.
Central and South American accounts should contact
Sales Manager, Stewart, Tabori & Chang.

EDITED BY
LINDA SUNSHINE with KRISTEN DOLAN,
ALISON HAGGE and JUDITH SUTTON

BOOK DESIGN BY
NAI Y. CHANG

PRODUCTION BY
ALICE WONG

Bugialli, Giuliano.
The best of Bugialli/
by Giuliano Bugialli; photographs by John Dominis
ISBN 1-55670-384-8
1. Cookery, Italian. I. Title.
TX723.B757   1994   94-16267
641.5945-DC20   CIP

Printed in Hong Kong
10   9   8   7   6   5   4   3   2   1

CONTENTS

INTRODUCTION

APPETIZERS

Pepper Salad with Capers	11	*Insalata di peperoni e capperi*
Wild Mushroom Tart	12	*Torta di funghi*
Bean Paste Canapés	15	*Crostini di fagioli*
Bruschetta with Arugula	16	*Bruschetta con ruchetta*
Marinated Capon Breast	18	*Insalata di cappone*
Mozzarella Grilled on Skewers Roman-Style	20	*Spiedini alla romano*
Egg-White Frittata	21	*Frittata di bianchi*
Bread Salad	23	*Panzanella del Valdarno*
Tomato Tart	24	*Torta di pomodoro*
Sage Batter Cake	26	*Salviata*

FIRST COURSES

Tagliatelle with Creamed Prosciutto Sauce	30	*Tagliatelle con dadi di prosciutto*
Saffron Pasta	32	*Pasta allo zafferano*
Parsley Pasta in Marjoram Cream Sauce	35	*Quadrucci alla maggiorana*
Tortelli Parma-Style	36	*Tortelli alla parmigiana o di erbette*
Green Lasagne Naples-Style	38	*Lasagne verdi alla napoletana*
Spaghetti with Air-Dried Cherry Tomatoes	40	*Spaghetti alla Sangiovannino*
Orecchiette with Cauliflower	43	*Orecchiette con cavolfiore*
Risotto Milan-Style	44	*Risotto alla milanese*
Polenta with Mascarpone and White Truffles	46	*Polenta con mascarpone e tartufi*
Grandmother's Kerchiefs (Stuffed Pasta Squares)	47	*Pezze della nonna*
Pasta with Zucchini and Shrimp	50	*Pasta alle zucchine con gamberi*
Peas and Paternostri	52	*Piselli e paternostri*
Minestrone Genoese-Style with Pesto Sauce	54	*Minestrone alla genovese*
Pasta with Savory Uncooked Vegetable Sauce	56	*Sedanini alla crudaiola in salsa piccante*
Bean-Barley Soup	57	*Fagioli ed orzo*
Fish Soup with Chopped Vegetables Livorno-Style	58	*Cacciucco con battuto alla livornese*
Pasta with Scallops in Fish Sauce	60	*Pasta al brodetto*
Macaroni Cooked in an Herbed Vegetable Sauce	62	*Pasta alle erbe alla napoletana*
Risotto with Sweet Bell Peppers	63	*Risotto ai peperoni*
Spaghetti with Cauliflower Sauce	64	*Spaghetti al sugo di cavolfiore*

BREADS

Bread from Prato 66 *Pane di Prato*
Schiacciata with Fresh Grapes 69 *Schiacciata con uva*
Focaccia with Basil 70 *Focaccia al basilico*
Rosemary Grissini 72 *Grissini al ramerino*

MAIN COURSES

Marinated Fried Sole Venetian-Style 76 *Sogliole in saor*
Rolled Stuffed Swordfish Cutlets on Skewers 78 *Involtini di pesce spada*
Scallops Chioggia-Style 80 *Canestrelli di Chioggia*
Carpaccio 81 *Carpaccio*
Ossobuco in a Vegetable Sauce 82 *Ossobuco alle verdure*
Chicken and Veal Galantine-Sausage with Green Peppercorns 84 *Salsiccia di pollo e vitella al pepe verde*
Chicken Roasted with Lemon Halves 86 *Pollo ai limoni*
Chicken Baked with Peppers 87 *Pollo ai peperoni al forno*
Roasted Veal Shank 88 *Stracotto di vitella alla fornarina*
Shrimp on Skewers with Thyme Sauce 90 *Spiedini di gamberi in salsa*
Cornmeal-Buckwheat Polenta with Pork Stew 92 *Polenta taragna con spezzatino di maiale*
Lamb with Herbed Horseradish Sauce 94 *Agnello alle erbe*

VEGETABLES

Eggplant Steaks 96 *Bistecche di melanzane*
Artichokes with Peas Roman-Style 97 *Carciofi e piselli alla romana*
Tuscan Beans Baked with Tuna and Lemon 99 *Fagioli stufati*
Stuffed Potato Focaccia 100 *Focaccia di patate*
Potatoes with Fennel 102 *Patate con finocchio*
Spicy Peperonata 104 *Peperonata all'arrabbiata*

DESSERTS

Orange Liqueur 106 *Liquore al mandarino*
Pears Stuffed with Cream and Chocolate 108 *Pere ripiene al cioccolato*
"Cooked Cream" Molds 110 *Panna cotta*
"Lift Me Up" 111 *Tiramisù*
Marsala Tart with Strawberries 112 *Torta al marsala con fragole*
Cherries Baked in Red Wine 114 *Ciliege al vino rosso*
Cherry Torte 115 *Torta di ciliege*
Marinated Whole Peaches with Mint 116 *Pesche alla menta*
Coffee-Nut Cake 117 *Dolce di caffè*
Lemon Timbales 118 *Limoni in forma*
Sautéed Fruit with Vanilla Sauce 120 *Frutta in padella con salsa alla vaniglia*

APPENDIX
INDEX

INTRODUCTION

What is "best" about this selection of my recipes? I would be a strange parent to prefer them to others—equally close to my heart—but over recent years, these are the ones that consistently prove to be the most popular and practiced. Included here, you will find recipes from my former books, the *Foods of Italy* and *Foods of Tuscany*, as well as from the many cooking classes—held in both my New York and Italian (*Cooking in Florence*) schools—and numerous demonstrations I give each year.

Previously unpublished recipes are gathered from all over Italy—from Friuli in the extreme north to Sicily in the extreme south with specimens from Emilia-Romagna, Calabria, Puglia, Tuscany, Campania, Lazio, Veneto, Lombardy and Piedmont. For the most part, I've excluded recipes that—little-known when I first published them—have become almost omnipresent. Fortunately, Italy possesses a culinary history of unfathomable depths. Great dishes have come to us from the Italian Renaissance, the wide array of regional cooking and from the *alta cucina*, cultivated in the old aristocratic courts, which absorbed vast traditions of ancient and medieval cuisines.

What determines an authentic or classic recipe? One approach, used by some cookbook authors, is to tally and edit recipes solicited from restaurants throughout Italy. Although this may seem logical, these recipes are often either watered-down versions to fit an individual restaurant's needs, or altogether misleading—restaurateurs may deliberately omit ingredients so as not to give away their secrets. When I research the origin and evolution of a dish, one source is not enough. I compare documented recipes (as early as the 14th century) with the many oral versions handed down from one generation to the next within a region's long-native families. Through this process, I believe the essence of a particular dish—its ingredients and preparation—is most fully revealed.

For me it is important to use these authentic ingredients and to eschew "creative" changes which bastardize the purity of the dish. For instance, I would never use corn starch in an Italian dessert because it is unknown in Italy. Most real Italian ingredients are now available abroad although it sometimes requires a little effort to obtain them. Occasionally, I give preference for an ingredient which is truly hard to find, but in such cases I do offer a second choice. My experience over some twenty years has been that many ingredients which were not imported when my earliest books were published are now easily available. It is really worth it not to take the easy way out; your reward is a more delicious dish.

Luckily, in addition to its best-known elements, authentic Italian cooking uses many ingredients not usually associated with it. The delicious *Polenta taragna* is made with buckwheat flour, as well as cornmeal, and served with a pork stew. *Agnello alle erbe* employs lambchops marinated in a variety of herbs and served with fresh horseradish. And barley, used whole—such as in the wonderful *Fagioli ed orzo* (bean-barley soup) included here—has a long history in Italy where it was first used by the Romans as a polenta and later, during the middle ages, when it was finely ground to make bread.

This collection offers a representative sampling of all the courses offered during the Italian meal: antipasti, first courses (fresh and dried pastas, soups and risotto), main courses (fish, meat and fowl), vegetable courses which are full-fledged dishes—not just side dishes—and a variety of desserts. Although some of the recipes are quite fashionable at the moment, I have not tailored them to fit contemporary trends.

Italian cooking preserves an age-old instinct for healthy eating through the use of many grains and vegetables and lighter fish and meats served in moderate quantities. Herbs are used extensively and even the most typical ones are unusually employed. In this collection: fresh sage forms the entire base for the batter cake, *Salviata*, fresh fennel bulbs are used to season the potatoes for *Patate con finocchio*, uncooked celery and herbs flavor the hot pasta in *Sedanini alla crudaiola in salsa piccante* and the pasta in *Pasta alle erbe alla napoletana* cooks in an exquisitely herbed sauce.

Flat breads called "focacce" have become exceedingly popular, and may be made of either potatoes or flour. I offer *Focaccia di patate*, a delicious bread stuffed with spicy peppers from Southern Italy. Other pepper dishes, so associated with all regions of Italy, include a spicy *Peperonata all'arrabbiata* from Rome and *Pollo ai peperoni al forno* in which the peppers dissolve to become sauce for the chicken. You will find a rare recipe from Livorno, the coastal city known for its fish soups, for *Cacciucco con battuto alla livornese* made with a variety of fish, shellfish and chopped vegetables. Fresh fruits are customarily served for dessert in Italy, while the more elaborate treats I present are more likely to be eaten only after special holiday meals in cafés. Three of my favorites are *Dolce di caffè* made of ground nuts, flavored with espresso and topped with coffee *zabaione*, *Torta di ciliege,* the wonderful cherry cake, and *Limoni in forma* individual molded timbales of lemon.

It has been rewarding to introduce so many people to the authentic Italian cooking in my classes. I hope the dishes in this book will reach an even greater group of food lovers. I try to give you, in all of them, my best.

GIULIANO BUGIALLI
MAY 1994

APPETIZERS

INSALATA DI PEPERONI E CAPPERI
Pepper Salad with Capers

1   large ripe tomato
1   medium-sized clove garlic, peeled
5   fresh basil leaves, torn into thirds
15   fresh mint leaves
4   tablespoons olive oil

    Salt and freshly ground black pepper
4   large sweet green or yellow bell peppers, or a combination of the two
2   tablespoons capers in wine vinegar, drained

Cut the tomato into pieces and pass the pieces through a food mill, using the disc with the smallest holes, into a small crockery or glass bowl.

Finely chop the garlic and add it to the bowl along with the basil and 5 of the mint leaves. Pour the oil over the herbs and add salt and pepper to taste. Mix very well with a wooden spoon. Cover the bowl with aluminum foil and refrigerate for 1 hour.

Preheat the oven to 375 degrees.

Place a baking dish with 4 cups of cold water on a lower shelf of the oven. After 5 minutes, put the whole peppers on the shelf above the steaming water.

Roast the peppers for about 40 minutes, turning them over three or four times.

Remove the peppers from the oven and put them in a plastic bag. Let them stand for 15 minutes.

Put the peppers in a large bowl of cold water and peel them, removing the stems and seeds.

Cut the peppers into thin strips. Arrange the strips on a serving dish and pour the prepared sauce over them. Mix very well and cover the dish with aluminum foil. Refrigerate for at least 1 hour.

Sprinkle the remaining mint leaves and the capers over the peppers and serve.

SERVES 6

OPPOSITE:
*A flowering caper bush grows from
the wall of a fourteenth-century monastery
above a plate of* Insalata di peperoni e capperi
(Pepper Salad with Capers).

TORTA DI FUNGHI
Wild Mushroom Tart

FOR THE CRUST

8   ounces unbleached all-purpose flour
8   tablespoons (4 ounces) sweet butter, at
    room temperature
    Pinch of salt
5   tablespoons cold water

FOR THE STUFFING

2   ounces dried *porcini* mushrooms
1   medium-sized red onion, cleaned

15 sprigs Italian parsley, leaves only
4   tablespoons olive oil
2   tablespoons (1 ounce) sweet butter
1   tablespoon tomato paste, preferably
    imported Italian
1   cup lukewarm beef broth, preferably
    homemade
    Salt and freshly ground black pepper
3   extra-large eggs
½   cup freshly grated *parmigiano-reggiano*

Prepare the crust: Sift the flour onto a board and arrange it in a mound. Cut the butter into pieces and place them over the mound. Let stand for ½ hour, or until the butter softens.

Start mixing the flour into the butter with your fingers; then rub the flour and butter between your palms until well mixed. Make a well in the center and put the salt and water in it. Start mixing with a fork, absorbing the flour-butter mixture. Then form a ball of dough with your hands. Knead gently until the dough becomes very smooth, about 2 minutes.

Slightly dampen a cotton dish towel and wrap the ball of dough in it. Let the dough rest in a cool place or on the bottom shelf of the refrigerator for at least 1 hour.

Meanwhile, prepare the stuffing: Soak the dried mushrooms in a bowl of lukewarm water for about ½ hour.

Finely chop the onion and parsley together on a board.

Heat the oil and butter in a heavy saucepan over medium heat and, when the butter is completely melted, add the chopped ingredients. Sauté gently for 10 minutes.

Drain the mushrooms, scraping away any sand that remains attached to them. Add the mushrooms to the pan and then add the tomato paste. Sauté for 5 minutes, stirring occasionally. Add the broth and season the mixture with salt and pepper. Cook slowly until almost all the broth has evaporated and the stuffing is thick and homogeneous, about 35 minutes. Remove the pan from the heat and transfer the stuffing to a crockery or glass bowl to cool completely, about 1 hour.

Butter a 9½-inch tart pan with a removable bottom.

Flour a pastry board. Unwrap the dough and knead it for about 1 minute on the board. Then use a rolling pin to roll out the dough to a round with a diameter of about 14 inches. Roll up the dough on the rolling pin and unroll it over the buttered pan. Gently press the dough into the bottom and up the sides of the pan. Cut off the dough around the rim of the pan by moving the rolling pin over it. Using a fork, make several punctures in the pastry to keep it from puffing up. Fit a sheet of wax paper or aluminum foil loosely over the pastry, then put weights or dried beans in the pan. Refrigerate the pastry for ½ hour.

Preheat the oven to 375 degrees.

Put the tart pan in the oven and bake for 40 minutes. Remove the pan from the oven, lift out the paper containing the weights and return the pan to the oven until the pastry is golden brown, 10 to 15 minutes longer.

Meanwhile, finish the stuffing: Add the eggs and *parmigiano-reggiano* to the cooled ingredients. Taste for salt and pepper and mix very well with a wooden spoon.

Remove the tart pan from the oven (leaving the oven on) and let the pastry cool in the pan on a rack for 10 minutes. Then pour the stuffing into the baked shell and return it to the oven for 20 minutes longer.

Remove the pan from the oven and let the tart cool for 15 minutes. Then transfer the tart from the pan to a serving platter. Slice it like a pie to serve. The tart may be eaten warm as a main dish or it may be served warm or at room temperature as an appetizer.

SERVES 8

CROSTINI DI FAGIOLI
Bean Paste Canapés

1 cup dried *cannellini* beans
½ teaspoon hot red pepper flakes
2 level teaspoons tomato paste, preferably imported Italian
Salt and freshly ground black pepper
1 medium-sized clove garlic, peeled
1 tablespoon rosemary leaves, fresh or preserved in salt or dried and blanched (see page 122)

1 cup chicken broth, preferably homemade
2 tablespoons (1 ounce) sweet butter
2 tablespoons olive oil
Juice of 1 lemon
16 pieces Tuscan bread or any other crusty, saltless bread, each 3 x 3 inches, ½ inch thick
10 sprigs Italian parsley, leaves only, finely chopped

Soak the beans overnight in a bowl of cold water.

The next morning, drain the beans and rinse them under cold running water. Put the beans in a small saucepan with 4½ cups water, half the hot red pepper flakes, the tomato paste and salt and pepper to taste. Put the pan over medium heat and cook, covered, for about 2 hours. (The cooking time for beans can vary a lot, depending on their dryness and the method that was used to dry them.) For this recipe, the beans are ready when almost all of the water has been absorbed and the beans are cooked through and very tender. Pass the beans and any remaining liquid through a food mill, using the disc with the medium-sized holes, into a small bowl.

Preheat the oven to 400 degrees.

Finely chop the garlic, rosemary and the remaining hot red pepper flakes together on a board.

Heat the broth to lukewarm in a small saucepan.

Heat the butter and oil in a second saucepan over medium heat and, when the butter is completely melted, add the chopped ingredients. Sauté for 2 minutes. Then add the bean purée and stir very well with a wooden spoon until all the ingredients are well amalgamated. Pour the heated broth into the bean paste, stir very well to incorporate it and cook for about 10 minutes longer, stirring every so often, until the texture is very smooth and fairly thick.

Meanwhile, put the bread on a baking sheet and heat it in the oven for 3 minutes.

Remove the bean paste from the heat, add the lemon juice and stir very well.

To make the canapés, spread 1 heaping tablespoon of the paste on each piece of bread. Arrange the *crostini* on a large serving platter, sprinkle the parsley over them and serve hot.

SERVES 8

15

BRUSCHETTA CON RUCHETTA
Bruschetta with Arugula

18 pieces Tuscan bread or any other crusty, saltless bread, each 3 x 2 inches, 1 inch thick

2 large ripe but not overripe tomatoes (about 1 pound total weight)

¼ pound *ruchetta* (arugula), cleaned and large stems removed

½ cup olive oil

Salt and freshly ground black pepper

Preheat the oven to 375 degrees.

Place the pieces of bread on a baking sheet or the shiny side of a piece of aluminum foil and toast them for about 10 minutes on each side. Arrange the toasted bread on a large platter.

Slice the tomatoes horizontally into 1-inch-thick slices, then cut each slice in half. Arrange the slices to cover the bread. Distribute the *ruchetta* over everything. Pour the oil over all and sprinkle with salt and pepper. Serve immediately.

SERVES 6

OPPOSITE:
In the shadow of the Benedictine abbey of San Vito near Bari, Bruschetta con ruchetta *(Bruschetta with Arugula) rests on the quay, surrounded by a variety of young field greens, which throughout southern Italy are eaten raw, as a salad, and served with cool white wine.*

INSALATA DI CAPPONE
Marinated Capon Breast

1   capon, about 4 pounds (yielding about
    1½ pounds breast meat)

TO BOIL THE CAPON
1   red onion, cleaned
1   celery stalk
1   carrot, scraped
5   sprigs Italian parsley
    Coarse-grained salt

FOR THE MARINADE
¾   cup olive oil
    Juice of 1 lemon
2   tablespoons red wine vinegar
3   whole cloves

2   bay leaves
3   tablespoons pignoli (pine nuts)
3   tablespoons raisins
    Salt and freshly ground black pepper
1   tablespoon granulated sugar
    A large pinch of hot red pepper flakes

TO SERVE
4   ripe but not overripe tomatoes
1   bunch chicory

OPTIONAL
    A few red radicchio leaves to be mixed
    with the chicory

Clean and wash the capon very well, removing all the fat from the cavity.

Bring 6 quarts cold water to a boil, then add the onion, celery, carrot and parsley. When the water comes to a boil again, add coarse-grained salt to taste and then the capon. Cook for 2 hours, removing the foam that rises to the top.

Remove the capon and transfer it to a large platter. Let rest until completely cold.

Remove the capon breast in two halves. Cut the breast meat into thick strips and put them in a large crockery or glass bowl (see Note).

Prepare the marinade: Pour the oil into a small crockery or glass bowl. Add the lemon juice. Then add the vinegar, cloves, bay leaves, pignoli and raisins, and season with salt and pepper to taste. Mix all the ingredients together with a wooden spoon. Pour the sauce over the capon breast strips and sprinkle with the sugar and hot red pepper flakes. Mix very well so that all the capon strips are well coated with the sauce. Transfer the contents of the bowl to a glass jar. Cover and refrigerate for at least 12 hours before serving.

When needed, remove the jar with the capon from the refrigerator and let stand until it reaches room temperature. Discard the bay leaves.

Cut the tomatoes into quarters and arrange them in a ring around the edge of a large platter. Arrange the chicory leaves and radicchio (if using) on the platter. Transfer the contents of the jar to the center of the platter and serve immediately.

SERVES 8

NOTE: The rest of the capon meat may be sautéed in 2 tablespoons of
olive oil with salt and pepper and served with a piquant sauce.

SPIEDINI ALLA ROMANA
Mozzarella Grilled on Skewers Roman-Style

1 thin loaf Italian bread
3 medium-sized *mozzarelle* (about 1½ pounds total weight)
3 tablespoons olive oil
 Salt and freshly ground black pepper
8 tablespoons (4 ounces) sweet butter

8 whole anchovies packed in salt, boned and rinsed, or 16 anchovy fillets packed in oil, drained

TO SERVE
4 sprigs Italian parsley

Cut the bread and the *mozzarelle* into ½-inch-thick slices. You will need 20 slices of bread and 16 slices of mozzarella.

Preheat the broiler to 375 degrees.

Thread the bread and cheese on 4 skewers, starting with the bread and alternating 5 slices of bread with 4 slices of cheese. Press the end slices toward the center so that everything is closely packed together. Place the skewers on an oiled baking sheet. Brush the slices of bread and cheese with 2 tablespoons of the oil and season them with salt and pepper. Put the baking sheet on the middle shelf of the preheated broiler, or 5 to 6 inches from the flame if you cannot regulate your broiler. Broil for about 15 minutes, checking the spiedini occasionally to make sure the bread does not burn.

Meanwhile, heat the butter and the remaining tablespoon of oil in a heavy saucepan over low heat. When the butter is completely melted, remove the pan from the heat. Add the anchovies and mash them with a fork until they are completely dissolved. Taste for salt and pepper.

Remove the skewers from the broiler, place each on an individual plate and pour some of the sauce over each serving. Accompany each with a sprig of parsley.

SERVES 4

FRITTATA DI BIANCHI
Egg-White Frittata

1   pound vegetable of your choice, such as carrots, string beans, celery, long beans or cauliflower, cleaned
    Coarse-grained salt
1   medium-sized clove garlic, peeled
10 sprigs Italian parsley, leaves only
4   tablespoons olive oil
    Salt and freshly ground black pepper
    A large pinch of hot red pepper flakes
6   extra-large egg whites

Cut the vegetable into pieces that measure less than 1 inch and soak them in a bowl of cold water for ½ hour.

Bring a medium-sized casserole of cold water to a boil over medium heat, then add coarse salt to taste. Drain the vegetable, add it to the casserole and cook until soft, 2 to 10 minutes, depending on the vegetable. Drain and cool under cold running water.

Finely chop the garlic and coarsely chop the parsley on a board.

Heat 3 tablespoons of the oil in a skillet over medium heat and, when the oil is warm, add the garlic and parsley. Sauté for 30 seconds. Add the cooled vegetable, season with salt and pepper and the hot red pepper flakes and sauté for 15 minutes, stirring with a wooden spoon. Transfer the sautéed vegetable to a crockery or glass bowl and let cool for ½ hour before using.

Prepare the frittata: Use a fork to lightly beat the egg whites in a crockery bowl. Add the cooled vegetable to the eggs and mix very well.

Heat the remaining tablespoon of oil in a 10-inch no-stick omelette pan over low heat. When the oil is hot, add the beaten eggs. As the eggs set in the pan, keep puncturing the bottom with a fork in order to allow the liquid on top to seep through to the bottom. When the eggs are set and the frittata is detached from the bottom of the pan, place a plate upside down over the pan and, holding the plate firmly, flip the plate and pan over so that the frittata comes out on the plate. Return the pan to the heat, carefully slide the frittata into the pan and cook the other side.

When the eggs are well set on the second side, about 1 minute, transfer the frittata to a serving dish. Serve hot or at room temperature.

SERVES 6

PANZANELLA DEL VALDARNO
Bread Salad

FOR THE SALAD

1 pound Tuscan bread or any other crusty, saltless bread, preferably whole wheat, several days old

6 tablespoons strong red wine vinegar

2 medium-sized red onions, cleaned

3 very large ripe tomatoes

1 celery heart

15 large fresh basil leaves, torn into thirds

TO DRESS THE SALAD

Salt and freshly ground black pepper

¾ cup olive oil

TO SERVE

15 large fresh basil leaves

OPTIONAL

4 whole anchovies packed in salt, boned and rinsed, or 8 anchovy fillets packed in oil, drained

Cut the bread into large pieces and place in a crockery or glass bowl. Pour 6 cups cold water and the vinegar over the bread. Soak the bread for ½ hour.

Meanwhile, cut the onions into small pieces and let rest in a bowl of cold water for ½ hour.

Cut the tomatoes into 2-inch pieces, without removing the seeds or skin, and place them in a large crockery or glass bowl. Cut the celery into small pieces and add it to the bowl with the tomatoes.

When ready, squeeze the liquid out of the bread and place the bread on top of the tomato-celery mixture. Do not mix. Drain the onions and scatter them over the bread, then sprinkle over the basil. Cover the bowl with plastic wrap and refrigerate for at least ½ hour.

Dress the salad with salt and pepper and the olive oil. Mix the salad very well and sprinkle on the basil leaves. If using the anchovies, coarsely chop them and add them at the last moment before serving.

SERVES 6

TORTA DI POMODORO
Tomato Tart

FOR THE CRUST
8 ounces unbleached all-purpose flour
8 tablespoons (4 ounces) cold sweet butter
5 tablespoons cold water
   Pinch of salt
   Pinch of freshly grated nutmeg

FOR THE FILLING
1 medium-sized celery stalk
1 carrot, scraped
1 medium-sized red onion, cleaned
1 small clove garlic, peeled
10 sprigs Italian parsley, leaves only
5 large fresh basil leaves

1½ pounds very ripe tomatoes or 1½
    pounds drained canned tomatoes,
    preferably imported Italian
2 tablespoons olive oil
2 tablespoons (1 ounce) sweet butter
   Salt and freshly ground black pepper
3 extra-large eggs
½ cup freshly grated *parmigiano-reggiano*

OPTIONAL
1 large very ripe tomato

TO SERVE
   Fresh basil leaves

Prepare the crust: Sift the flour onto a board and arrange it in a mound. Cut the butter into pieces and place over the mound. Use a metal dough scraper to incorporate the butter into the flour, adding the water 1 tablespoon at a time and seasoning with the salt and nutmeg. When all the water is used up, a ball of dough should be formed. Place the ball in a dampened cotton dish towel and refrigerate for at least 2 hours before using. (Or, leave the crust in the refrigerator overnight.)

Prepare the filling: Coarsely chop the celery, carrot, onion, garlic, parsley and basil all together on a board.

If using fresh tomatoes, cut them into large pieces. Place the fresh or canned tomatoes in a non-reactive casserole, then arrange all the prepared vegetables over the tomatoes. Pour the olive oil on top. Cover the casserole, set it over medium heat and cook for about 1 hour, without stirring, shaking the casserole often to be sure the tomatoes do not stick to the bottom.

Pass the contents of the casserole through a food mill, using the disc with the smallest holes, into a second casserole. Add the butter and season with salt and pepper.

Place the casserole over medium heat and let the mixture reduce for 15 minutes more, or until a rather thick sauce forms. Transfer the sauce to a crockery or glass bowl and let cool completely.

Butter a 9½-inch tart pan with a removable bottom.

Flour a pastry board. Unwrap the pastry and knead it for about 30 seconds on the board, then use a rolling pin to roll out the dough to a 14-inch disc. Roll up the disc on the rolling pin and unroll it over the buttered pan. Gently press the dough into the bottom and up the sides of the pan. Cut off the dough around the rim of the pan by moving the rolling pin over it. Using a fork, make several punctures in the pastry to keep it from puffing up. Fit a piece of aluminum foil loosely over the pastry, then put pie weights or dried beans in the pan. Refrigerate the pastry for ½ hour.

Preheat the oven to 375 degrees.

Place the tart pan in the oven and bake for 35 minutes. Remove the pan from the oven and lift out the foil and weights or beans. Return the pan to the oven and bake until the crust is golden, about 10 minutes.

Meanwhile, finish preparing the filling: Add the eggs and *parmigiano-reggiano* to the cooled tomato sauce. Taste for salt and pepper and mix very well with a wooden spoon.

Remove the tart pan from the oven (leaving the oven on). Let the crust cool for 15 minutes, then pour in the prepared filling. If desired, very thinly slice the tomato, remove all the seeds and arrange the slices over the filling.

Bake the tart for 20 minutes longer. Remove the pan from the oven and let the tart cool for 15 minutes before transferring it from the tart pan to a serving dish. Slice the tart like a pie and serve it with the fresh basil leaves.

SERVES 6 TO 8

SALVIATA
Sage Batter Cake

FOR THE CAKE
½ cup freshly grated *parmigiano-reggiano*
6 tablespoons unbleached all-purpose flour
2 whole extra-large eggs
6 extra-large eggs, separated
1 cup milk
Salt and freshly ground black pepper
Freshly grated nutmeg

25 large fresh sage leaves

TO BAKE THE CAKE
4 tablespoons (2 ounces) sweet butter

TO SERVE
3 tablespoons freshly grated *parmigiano-reggiano*
Fresh sage leaves

Prepare the cake: Place the *parmigiano-reggiano*, flour, whole eggs, egg yolks and milk in a bowl and stir together with a wooden spoon. Season with salt and pepper and nutmeg and let stand for at least ½ hour in a cool place or on the bottom shelf of the refrigerator.

Meanwhile, coarsely chop the sage on a board.

Preheat the oven to 375 degrees. Use the 4 tablespoons of butter to heavily butter the bottom and sides of a 13½-by-8¾-inch glass baking dish.

When the batter is ready, place the buttered baking dish in the oven for 10 minutes.

Meanwhile, with a wire whisk, beat the egg whites in a copper bowl, until stiff. Then quickly fold them into the batter together with the chopped sage.

Remove the baking dish from the oven and pour off all of the melted butter. Then pour the batter into the warmed dish and bake for ½ hour.

Remove the cake from the oven and serve hot, cut into squares, with the *parmigiano-reggiano* and fresh sage leaves sprinkled all over.

SERVES 8

OPPOSITE:
The aromatic leaves of sage.

26

FIRST COURSES

TAGLIATELLE CON DADI DI PROSCIUTTO
Tagliatelle with Creamed Prosciutto Sauce

FOR THE PASTA
4   cups unbleached all-purpose flour
5   extra-large eggs
    Pinch of salt

TO COOK THE PASTA
    Coarse-grained salt

FOR THE SAUCE
4   ounces very lean prosciutto, in one piece
8   tablespoons (4 ounces) sweet butter
1½ cups heavy cream
    Salt and freshly ground black pepper
    Pinch of freshly grated nutmeg
¾   cup freshly grated *parmigiano-reggiano*

Prepare the pasta, following the instructions on pages 122-123. Stretch the pasta to a thickness of less than ¹/₁₆ inch, by hand or using a pasta machine. Cut it into strips ¼ inch wide. Put the pasta on cotton dish towels to rest until needed.

Bring a large pot of cold water to a boil, and add coarse-grained salt to taste.

Meanwhile, prepare the sauce: Cut the prosciutto into cubes a little smaller than ½ inch.

Melt the butter in a large casserole over low heat. Add the prosciutto and sauté it lightly for 1 minute.

Remove from the heat.

Add the pasta to the boiling water and cook for 30 seconds to 1 minute, depending on the dryness of the pasta. Drain the pasta and add it to the casserole with the prosciutto and butter.

Immediately pour the cream over the pasta and season with salt and pepper and the nutmeg. Gently mix all the ingredients together, then add the cheese and mix again. Transfer to a warm serving dish and serve immediately.

SERVES 8

Tagliatelle con dadi di prosciutto
(Tagliatelle with Creamed Prosciutto Sauce)
is presented in a hollowed-out wheel of
parmigiano-reggiano.

PASTA ALLO ZAFFERANO
Saffron Pasta

FOR THE SAUCE

3 medium-sized leeks or 3 medium-sized red onions, cleaned
4 tablespoons olive oil
2 tablespoons (1 ounce) sweet butter
1 ossobuco (1½-inch slice of veal shank, with bone and marrow)
1 tablespoon unbleached all-purpose flour
½ medium-sized red onion, cleaned
1 small celery stalk
1 small carrot, scraped
1 strip lemon rind (about 2 inches long)
1 cup dry white wine
3 cups canned imported Italian tomatoes, drained
1 tablespoon tomato paste, preferably imported Italian
Salt and freshly ground black pepper

PLUS

1 large clove garlic, peeled
15 sprigs Italian parsley, leaves only
4 sage leaves, fresh or preserved in salt (see page 122)
Grated peel of 1 lemon

FOR THE PASTA

4 cups unbleached all-purpose flour
5 extra-large eggs
Pinch of salt
1 scant teaspoon powdered saffron or one ⅛-gram package saffron threads, finely ground

TO COOK THE PASTA

Coarse-grained salt

TO SERVE

2 tablespoons (1 ounce) sweet butter

Prepare the sauce: If using leeks, cut off the ends of the leeks with the attached roots. Then cut off the stems at the point where the white color turns green. Slice the remaining white stems into rings less than ½ inch wide. Put the rings in a bowl of cold water and let them soak for ½ hour, or until all the sand is removed.

Heat the oil and butter in a casserole over medium heat. When the butter is completely melted, drain the leeks and add them to the casserole. Sauté for 5 minutes.

Tie the ossobuco with string to keep it together while it cooks. Use the tablespoon of flour to lightly flour the ossobuco on both sides.

Add the meat to the casserole and sauté until it is golden brown on both sides, about 4 minutes on each side.

Meanwhile, finely chop the onion, celery, carrot and lemon rind together on a board.

Add the chopped ingredients to the casserole and sauté for 2 minutes longer. Add the wine and let it evaporate over low heat for 20 minutes. Add the canned tomatoes and the tomato paste, cover the casserole and simmer for 40 minutes, stirring occasionally. Taste for salt and pepper. Turn the ossobuco, cover the casserole again and simmer for 25 minutes longer. Transfer the meat to a board and remove the string and the bone.

ABOVE: *Saffron is traditionally ground into a powder with a marble mortar and pestle. The marble has just enough friction to grind the soft threads of the saffron without absorbing the powder.* LEFT: *In* Pasta allo zafferano *(Saffron Pasta) the bright-yellow, freshly-made pasta is served with a veal sauce.*

Pass the contents of the casserole and the ossobuco meat through a food mill, using the disc with the medium-sized holes, into a second casserole. Simmer the sauce, uncovered, over medium heat for about 15 minutes. Taste for salt and pepper. Remove the casserole from the heat and let it stand, covered, until needed.

Finely chop the garlic, parsley and sage together on a board. Transfer the chopped ingredients to a small crockery or glass bowl. Add the grated lemon peel and mix all the ingredients together with a wooden spoon. Cover the bowl and let stand until needed.

Prepare the pasta, following the instructions on pages 122-123, grinding the saffron with a marble mortar and pestle, and adding it to the well in the flour together with the eggs and salt. Stretch the pasta to a thickness of less than $1/16$ inch, by hand or using a pasta machine. Cut the pasta sheet into ¼-inch-wide *tagliatelle* strips. Put the cut pasta on cotton dish towels to rest until needed.

Bring a large pot of cold water to a boil, and add coarse-grained salt to taste.

Melt the butter on a large serving platter placed over the pot of boiling water. Reheat the sauce.

When the butter is melted, remove the platter and add the pasta to the boiling water. Cook for 40 seconds to 1 minute, depending on the dryness of the pasta. Drain the pasta and transfer it to the serving platter with the melted butter. Pour the sauce over the pasta and toss very well, then sprinkle with the chopped aromatic herbs in the small bowl and serve immediately.

SERVES 8

A delicate sheet of pasta, stretched with a manual machine, shows the whole parsley leaf in the pasta itself.

QUADRUCCI ALLA MAGGIORANA
Parsley Pasta in Marjoram Cream Sauce

FOR THE PASTA
4 cups unbleached all-purpose flour
4 extra-large eggs
4 teaspoons olive oil or vegetable oil
   Pinch of salt
30 large sprigs Italian parsley, leaves only

TO COOK THE PASTA
   Coarse-grained salt

FOR THE SAUCE
8 tablespoons (4 ounces) sweet butter
2 large cloves garlic, peeled but left whole
1½ cups heavy cream
   Salt and freshly ground black pepper
1 tablespoon dried marjoram

TO SERVE
8 tablespoons freshly grated *parmigiano-reggiano*

Prepare the pasta, following the instructions on pages 122-123. Stretch the pasta to a thickness of ⅛ inch, by hand or using a pasta machine.

Place the whole parsley leaves on top of half the length of the sheet of pasta. Fold the other half of the sheet of pasta over the parsley, and press the pasta together. Continue to roll out the sheet of pasta until it is ¹⁄₁₆ inch thick. Using a scalloped pastry cutter, cut the pasta into squares of about 2 inches. Let the pasta rest on paper towels until needed.

Bring a large pot of cold water to a boil, and add coarse-grained salt to taste.

Meanwhile, prepare the sauce: Place a large skil-let with the butter over medium heat and, when the butter is melted, add the garlic. Sauté for 2 minutes, or until lightly golden. Discard the garlic, and keep the butter warm.

Add the pasta to the boiling water and cook it for 2 to 3 minutes, depending on the dryness of the pasta.

Drain the pasta, add it to the skillet and mix well. Add the cream and salt and pepper to taste, then the marjoram. Cook, continuously stirring with a wooden spoon, until all the cream is absorbed by the pasta, about 1 minute. Serve immediately, sprin-kling each dish with the *parmigiano-reggiano*.

SERVES 8

35

TORTELLI ALLA PARMIGIANA O DI ERBETTE
Tortelli Parma-Style

FOR THE STUFFING
2   pounds Swiss chard
1   pound spinach
    Coarse-grained salt
15 ounces whole-milk ricotta
4   extra-large eggs
6   ounces *parmigiano-reggiano*, freshly grated
4   tablespoons (2 ounces) sweet butter, at
    room temperature
    Salt and freshly ground black pepper
    Freshly grated nutmeg

FOR THE PASTA
4   cups unbleached all-purpose flour
5   extra-large eggs
    Pinch of salt

TO COOK THE PASTA
    Coarse-grained salt

FOR THE SAUCE
16 tablespoons (8 ounces) sweet butter
1   cup freshly grated *parmigiano-reggiano*

Prepare the stuffing: Wash the Swiss chard and spinach carefully, removing the large stems.

Bring a large pot of cold water to a boil. Add coarse-grained salt and then the greens. Cook for 10 minutes, then drain and cool under cold running water. Squeeze dry, and finely chop the cooked greens on a board.

Put the ricotta in a large bowl and add the eggs, chopped greens, *parmigiano-reggiano* and butter. Season with salt and pepper and nutmeg. Mix all the ingredients together with a wooden spoon to obtain a smooth texture. Cover the bowl and refrigerate until needed.

Prepare the pasta, following the instructions on pages 122-123. Stretch the layer of pasta to a thickness of slightly less than 1/16 inch, by hand or using a pasta machine.

To make the *tortelli*, starting 1 inch from the top and side edges of the sheet of pasta, make two lengthwise rows of filling dots, each 2 inches apart; use ½ tablespoon of the filling for each dot. Continue the two-row sequence halfway down the sheet of pasta. Fold over the other half of the sheet of pasta and quickly press down around the dots of filling. Use a scalloped pastry wheel to cut out 2-inch squares, and seal them all around (see Note).

Bring a large pot of cold water to a boil and add coarse-grained salt to taste.

Meanwhile, melt the butter for the sauce in a double boiler or *bagnomarìa*.

Add the *tortelli* to the boiling water and cook for 1 to 2 minutes, depending on the dryness of the pasta.

Pour ¼ cup of the melted butter onto a large serving dish. With a skimmer-strainer, transfer the *tortelli* from the pot onto the prepared dish, sprinkling some *parmigiano-reggiano* and pouring some melted butter over each layer. Serve hot.

SERVES 8

NOTE: It is best to stuff the pasta while it is still very fresh. If it has dried a bit, moisten the edges with water or beaten egg white to seal.

The sixteenth-century church of the Madonna della Steccata in Parma
is a splendid example of the Classical style. The celebrated pasta dish
of Parma, Tortelli alla parmigiana (Tortelli Parma-Style), is served on a
terrace overlooking the church.

LASAGNE VERDI ALLA NAPOLETANA
Green Lasagne Naples-Style

FOR THE PASTA
3½ cups unbleached all-purpose flour
2   extra-large eggs
2   teaspoons olive oil or vegetable oil
1   heaping tablespoon finely chopped boiled
    spinach (from ½ pound fresh spinach leaves,
    stems removed)
    Pinch of salt

TO COOK THE PASTA
    Coarse-grained salt
2   tablespoons olive oil or vegetable oil

FOR THE TOMATO SAUCE
4   tablespoons olive oil
3   cloves garlic, peeled but left whole
2¾ pounds ripe tomatoes or canned imported

Italian tomatoes, drained
Salt and freshly ground black pepper

FOR THE RICOTTA STUFFING
15 ounces ricotta
4   tablespoons freshly grated *parmigiano-reggiano*
4   tablespoons (2 ounces) sweet butter, at room
    temperature
    Salt and freshly ground black pepper
    Pinch of freshly grated nutmeg

FOR THE MOZZARELLA STUFFING
8   ounces whole-milk mozzarella
    Salt and freshly ground black pepper

PLUS
20 fresh basil leaves (see Note)

Prepare the pasta, following the instructions on pages 122-123, placing the chopped spinach in the well in the flour together with the other ingredients. Stretch the pasta to a thickness of slightly less than ¹⁄₁₆ inch, by hand or using a pasta machine. Use a scalloped pastry wheel to cut the sheets of pasta into squares of about 5 inches. Put the cut pasta on cotton dish towels to rest until needed.

Bring a large pot of cold water to a boil, and add coarse-grained salt to taste.

Precook the pasta squares in the boiling water for 5 seconds after the water returns to a boil. Then transfer them to a large bowl of cold water to which the olive oil has been added. When all the pasta squares have been boiled, lay them in a single layer on dampened cotton dish towels. Cover the pasta squares with additional dampened cotton dish towels.

Prepare the tomato sauce: Put the oil and garlic in a saucepan over medium heat. Sauté the garlic for 1 minute, or until very light golden brown. Add the tomatoes, lower the heat, cover the saucepan and simmer for about 25 minutes (see Note). Taste for salt and pepper. Pass the contents of the pan through a food mill, using the disc with the smallest holes, into another pan and put the sauce back over medium heat. Cook, uncovered, to reduce for 15 minutes longer. Transfer the sauce to a crockery or glass bowl and let it cool completely, about 1 hour. The sauce may be prepared as much as a day in advance.

Prepare the cheese stuffings: Put the ricotta in a

LEFT: *Nearly ready for baking, the lasagne reveals its next-to-top layer of tomatoes and basil. The green pasta of the bottom layer still hangs over the sides; it will be folded over* the top and a final layer of tomatoes and basil will be added. RIGHT: *The finished* Lasagne verdi alla napoletana *(Green Lasagne Naples-Style).*

bowl. Add the *parmigiano-reggiano*, butter, salt and pepper to taste and the nutmeg. Mix all the ingredients together with a wooden spoon.

Grate the mozzarella with a coarse grater and put it in a separate bowl. Season it with salt and pepper.

Preheat the oven to 375 degrees.

To assemble the dish, heavily oil a 13½-by-8¾-inch baking dish. Then fit in enough pasta squares to cover the bottom of the baking dish and to allow about 1 inch of the pasta to hang over all around the edges of the dish. Cover the pasta on the bottom of the dish with a quarter of the tomato sauce. Sprinkle a quarter of the basil leaves over the sauce (see Note). Add another layer of pasta to just cover the tomato sauce, but with no overhanging pasta. Cover this second layer of pasta with one third of the ricotta mixture. Then make another layer of pasta and top it with one third of the grated mozzarella. Keep making layers of pasta, alternating in between them the three different fillings in the same order, finishing with a layer of mozzarella covered with 3 pasta squares. Fold the ends of the pasta squares, hanging over the edges of the baking dish, over the top of the last 3 pasta squares. Pour the remaining tomato sauce over the top of the pasta. Sprinkle the remaining basil leaves over the tomato sauce.

Place the dish in the oven and bake for 25 minutes. Remove the dish from the oven and let it sit for 15 minutes before serving.

SERVES 8 TO 10

NOTE: If fresh basil is not available and basil preserved in salt (see page 122) is substituted, add the basil leaves to the tomato sauce while it is cooking. Remove them before passing the sauce through the food mill.

SPAGHETTI ALLA SANGIOVANNINO
Spaghetti with Air-Dried Cherry Tomatoes

FOR THE SAUCE
1 pound ripe cherry tomatoes
3 cloves garlic, peeled
½ cup olive oil
  Salt and freshly ground black pepper
1 teaspoon hot red pepper flakes

TO COOK THE PASTA
  Coarse-grained salt
1 pound dried spaghetti, preferably
  imported Italian

PLUS
25 sprigs Italian parsley, leaves only

Prepare the sauce: Preheat the oven to 375 degrees.

Put the cherry tomatoes on a baking sheet and bake for 5 minutes.

Remove the tomatoes from the oven and let them cool for 10 minutes. Then cut the tomatoes in half, retaining the seeds and skin.

Coarsely chop the garlic on a board.

Heat the oil in a large casserole over medium heat. Add the garlic and sauté for 2 minutes, then raise the heat to very high and add the tomatoes. Sauté for 5 minutes longer. (Even over very high heat, the tomatoes will not dissolve completely.) Season with salt and pepper to taste and the hot red pepper flakes.

Meanwhile, bring a large pot of cold water to a boil, and add coarse-grained salt to taste.

Add the pasta to the boiling water, stir with a wooden spoon and cover the pot to bring the water back to a boil as quickly as possible. Remove the lid and cook the pasta until it is al dente (9 to 12 minutes, depending on the brand).

Drain the pasta and transfer it to the casserole with the sauce. Sprinkle the parsley over all, mix very well and serve immediately. (No cheese should be used with this dish.)

OPPOSITE:
Bunches of plump cherry tomatoes, tied with a string, dry in the warm air of southern Italy.

SERVES 4 TO 6

ORECCHIETTE CON CAVOLFIORE
Orecchiette with Cauliflower

FOR THE CAULIFLOWER

1 large cauliflower, about 2½ pounds, green leaves removed
  Coarse-grained salt
2 large cloves garlic, peeled but left whole
¾ cup olive oil
5 whole anchovies packed in salt, boned and rinsed, or 10 anchovy fillets packed in oil, drained
20 sprigs Italian parsley, leaves only
  Salt and freshly ground black pepper

FOR THE PASTA

1 pound dried *orecchiette*, preferably imported Italian, or fresh *orecchiette* made with the following ingredients:
1 cup semolina flour
2 cups unbleached all-purpose flour
1 cup cold water
  Pinch of salt

OPTIONAL

½ teaspoon hot red pepper flakes

Put the cauliflower in a large bowl of cold water and soak for ½ hour.

Meanwhile, if you are making fresh *orecchiette*, follow the instructions on pages 122-123 for making the dough, placing the water and salt in the well of the combined flours. To shape the pasta, roll the dough into a long cord and cut into ½-inch discs. Flatten each disc with your thumb, then turn your thumb clockwise to make the orecchiette, or "little ear" shape.

Bring a large pot of cold water to a boil, and add coarse-grained salt to taste.

Cut the cauliflower into florets, discarding the stems. Put the florets into the boiling water along with the garlic. Cook for 3 minutes. Drain the cauliflower, reserving the cooking water. Transfer the cauliflower to a bowl until needed. Discard the garlic.

Heat the oil in a large casserole over medium heat and, when the oil is warm, remove the casserole from the heat and add the anchovy fillets. Mash them with a fork.

Finely chop the parsley on a board.

Meanwhile, bring the cauliflower cooking water back to a boil.

Add the pasta to the boiling water. If you are using the fresh *orecchiette*, cook it for 5 to 10 minutes, depending on the dryness of the pasta. (For further details, see *Giuliano Bugialli's Classic Techniques of Italian Cooking.*) If you are using dried pasta, cook it until it is al dente (9 to 12 minutes, depending on the brand).

Drain the pasta and transfer it to the casserole with the anchovies. Put the casserole back over medium heat, stir very well and add the cooked cauliflower. Taste for salt and pepper, mix all the ingredients together and cook for 1 minute longer. If using the hot red pepper flakes, add them. Sprinkle with the parsley and serve immediately.

SERVES 6

RISOTTO ALLA MILANESE
Risotto Milan-Style

FOR THE RISOTTO

8 cups beef broth, preferably homemade
3½ pounds veal or beef bones from the upper
    leg, cut into pieces
1 medium-sized white onion, cleaned
6 tablespoons (3 ounces) sweet butter
2 cups raw rice, preferably Italian *Arborio*
½ cup dry white wine

About 30 saffron threads
Salt and freshly ground black pepper

PLUS

2 tablespoons (1 ounce) sweet butter
½ cup freshly grated *parmigiano-reggiano*

OPTIONAL

6 tablespoons freshly grated *parmigiano- reggiano*

Heat the broth in a large casserole. When it comes to a boil, add the bones and simmer for 20 minutes. Take the casserole off the heat. Remove the bones and put them on a board. Using a long-handled fork, carefully lift out the marrow from each bone and put it on a plate. Discard the bones.

Wet a piece of heavy cheesecloth or a cotton dish towel and chill it in the freezer for 5 minutes. Then stretch the cheesecloth over a colander and strain the broth through it to remove any impurities. (You will have ample strained broth to prepare the risotto, as only about 4½ cups are needed.)

Cut the marrow into small pieces. Finely chop the onion on a board.

Heat the butter in a heavy casserole over low heat and, when the butter is melted, add the marrow and then the chopped onion. Sauté until the onion is translucent, about 4 minutes. Then add the rice and sauté for 4 minutes. Add the wine and let it evaporate, about 3 minutes.

Meanwhile, reheat the broth. Start adding it, a little at a time, to the casserole, stirring continuously and gently each time. Do not add additional broth until the broth previously added has been completely absorbed. After the first cup of broth has been added, measure out 3½ cups of broth and add the saffron to it. The broth must continue to boil in order to dissolve the saffron threads. Season the rice with salt and pepper. Keep adding broth until the rice is cooked but still al dente. (It will take about 18 minutes from the time the first broth is added.)

Remove the casserole from the heat, add the butter and *parmigiano-reggiano* and mix very well with a wooden spoon until the butter is completely melted and the cheese absorbed. Serve with additional *parmigiano-reggiano*, if desired.

SERVES 6

POLENTA CON MASCARPONE E TARTUFI
Polenta with Mascarpone and White Truffles

1 medium-sized fresh or canned white truffles
2 tablespoons (1 ounce) sweet butter
8 heaping tablespoons *mascarpone*

3 quarts beef broth, preferably homemade
Coarse-grained salt
1 pound coarse or stone-ground Italian yellow cornmeal

If the truffle is fresh, clean it very carefully with a truffle brush to remove all of the sand.

Use the 2 tablespoons of butter to lightly butter eight dinner plates. Put 1 heaping tablespoon of *mascarpone* in the center of each plate. Put the plates in the refrigerator until needed.

Bring the broth to a boil in a large pot over medium heat, and add coarse-grained salt to taste. Then start pouring in the cornmeal in a very slow stream, stirring continuously with a flat wooden spoon. Be sure to pour the cornmeal slowly and to keep stirring, or the polenta will easily become very lumpy. Stir slowly, without stopping, for 45 to 50 minutes from the moment the last of the cornmeal is added to the pot. If some lumps form, push them against the side of the pot to crush them with the spoon.

When the polenta is cooked, taste it for salt, and then remove the pot from the heat. Immediately ladle some of the polenta over the cheese on the prepared plates. The polenta should cover the cheese completely. Use a truffle cutter to slice the truffle over the polenta on the plates. Serve immediately.

SERVES 8

46

PEZZE DELLA NONNA
Grandmother's Kerchiefs (Stuffed Pasta Squares)

FOR THE *POMMAROLA* SAUCE
1 medium-sized red onion, cleaned
1 medium-sized celery stalk
1 large clove garlic, peeled
1 medium-sized carrot, scraped
10 sprigs Italian parsley, leaves only
8 large basil leaves, fresh or preserved in
   salt (see page 122)
2 pounds very ripe tomatoes or 2 pounds
   drained canned tomatoes,
   preferably imported Italian
2 tablespoons olive oil
2 tablespoons (1 ounce) sweet butter
   Salt and freshly ground black pepper

FOR THE *BALSAMELLA*
8 tablespoons (4 ounces) sweet butter
4 tablespoons unbleached all-purpose flour
3½ cups milk
   Pinch of salt

FOR THE STUFFING
2½ pounds spinach, cleaned and large
   stems removed

   Coarse-grained salt
1 pound ricotta, drained very well
1 extra-large egg
3 extra-large egg yolks
1 cup freshly grated *parmigiano-reggiano*
   Salt and freshly ground black pepper
   Freshly grated nutmeg

FOR THE PASTA
2¼ cups unbleached all-purpose flour
4 extra-large egg yolks
¼ cup cold water
2 tablespoons olive oil or vegetable oil
   Pinch of salt

TO COOK THE PASTA
   Coarse-grained salt
2 tablespoons vegetable oil or olive oil

PLUS
2 tablespoons (1 ounce) sweet butter

TO SERVE
   Large fresh basil leaves

Prepare the *pommarola* sauce: Very coarsely chop the onion, celery, garlic, carrot, parsley and basil all together on a board.

If using fresh tomatoes, cut them into large pieces. Place the fresh or canned tomatoes in a medium-sized nonreactive casserole and add the chopped vegetables and oil. Do not mix. Cover the casserole, set over low heat and cook for 1½ hours without stir-ring, shaking the casserole every so often to prevent the tomatoes from sticking to the bottom.

Pass the contents of the casserole through a food mill, using the disc with the smallest holes, into a second casserole. Place the sauce over medium heat and add the butter and salt and pepper to taste. Mix very well and let reduce for 15 minutes, stirring every so often with a wooden spoon. When ready, transfer the sauce to a crockery or glass bowl and let stand until needed. The sauce can be prepared up to two days in advance and stored, covered, in the refrigerator.

Prepare the *balsamella* : Melt the butter over low heat in a heavy (preferably copper or enamel) saucepan. When the butter starts to froth, add all of the flour, in one addition, and stir with a wooden spoon. Continuing to stir, cook the mixture until the flour is completely incorporated, 1 to 3 minutes. If any lumps form, use the wooden spoon to crush them against the side of the pan. Remove the mixture from the heat and let stand for the time it takes for the milk to reach a boil.

Pour the milk into another saucepan and heat until it comes almost to the boiling point. Place the pan with the butter-flour mixture over low heat and, all at once, add the nearly boiling milk and stir until smooth. Continue to cook the sauce over low heat and, when it starts to boil, add the salt. Cook, stirring gently, for about 10 minutes. Transfer the *balsamella* to a crockery or glass bowl and press a piece of buttered waxed paper over it to prevent a skin from forming.

Prepare the stuffing: Soak the spinach in a bowl of cold water for ½ hour.

Bring a large pot of cold water to a boil over medium heat, and add coarse salt to taste. Drain the spinach, add it to the pot and boil for 5 minutes.

Drain the spinach and cool under cold running water. Squeeze the spinach (not absolutely dry) and finely chop it on a board.

Place the spinach, ricotta, egg, egg yolks and *parmigiano-reggiano* in a crockery or glass bowl and mix very well. Season with salt and pepper and nutmeg, mix again, cover and refrigerate until needed.

Prepare the pasta, following the instructions on pages 122-123. Stretch the layer of pasta to a thickness of a little less than $1/16$ of an inch, by hand or using a pasta machine. Cut the pasta sheet into 6-inch lasagne squares.

Meanwhile, bring another large pot of cold water to a boil, and add coarse-grained salt to taste.

Precook the lasagne squares in the boiling water for a few seconds, then transfer them to a bowl of cold water to which the oil has been added. Remove the squares from the water and let rest on dampened cotton dish towels until needed.

Preheat the oven to 375 degrees. Use the 2 tablespoons of butter to grease an ovenproof 15-inch round baking dish or a 13½-by-8¾-inch glass baking pan.

Place 2 heaping tablespoons of the stuffing in the center of each pasta square. Fold each one into a triangle, then take the two bottom points and fold them over to meet in the center of the triangle. Without pressing on them, gently transfer the stuffed *pezze* into the prepared dish, arranging them to form two circles, one inside the other, with the points toward the middle.

Pour the *balsamella* over the *pezze* and bake for 20 minutes.

Meanwhile, reheat the tomato sauce.

When ready, place one or two *pezze* on each plate and pour some of the reheated tomato sauce over the unstuffed part of each *pezza*. Add a basil leaf to each plate.

SERVES 8 OR 16

PASTA ALLE ZUCCHINE CON GAMBERI
Pasta with Zucchini and Shrimp

FOR THE SAUCE

2   small zucchini (about 10 ounces total
    weight), cleaned
    Coarse-grained salt
½   pound small shrimp, unshelled (if
    shrimp are not small, cut into halves)
1   lemon
1   large clove garlic, peeled
4   tablespoons olive oil
    A large pinch of ground saffron
1   cup very warm chicken or meat broth,
    preferably homemade
    Salt and freshly ground black pepper

FOR THE PASTA
3½ cups unbleached all-purpose flour

1   extra-large egg
2   extra-large egg yolks
½   cup cold water
    Pinch of salt
1   tablespoon olive oil or vegetable oil

TO COOK THE PASTA
    Coarse-grained salt

PLUS
1   large very ripe tomato, blanched, peeled,
    seeded and cut into ½-inch squares

TO SERVE
15 sprigs Italian parsley, leaves only

Cut the zucchini into discs not more than ½ inch thick. Let them stand for ½ hour in a bowl of cold water to which coarse salt has been added. Place the shrimp in a bowl of cold water with coarse salt and the lemon cut in half and squeezed, and soak for ½ hour.

Prepare the pasta, following the instructions on pages 122-123. Stretch the pasta sheet to a thickness of ⅛ inch, by hand or using a pasta machine. Cut into spaghetti by hand or by machine. Let the pasta rest on cotton towels until needed.

Bring a large pot of cold water to a boil, and add coarse-grained salt to taste.

Meanwhile, prepare the sauce: Drain the zucchini and rinse under cold running water. Drain the shrimp, then shell and devein them, if needed.

Coarsely chop the garlic.

Place a skillet with the oil over low heat. When the oil is warm, add the garlic. Sauté for 2 minutes. Dissolve the saffron in the broth. Add the zucchini to the skillet and sauté for 30 seconds, then raise the heat to high, season with salt and pepper and add all the broth. Cover the skillet and cook for 2 minutes, stirring every so often with a wooden spoon.

Add the pasta to the boiling water and cook it for 1 to 3 minutes, depending on the dryness of the pasta.

While the pasta is cooking, add the shrimp and tomato to the skillet, mix well and cook for 2 minutes more.

Drain the pasta, add it to the skillet, sprinkle on the parsley and mix gently. Serve hot.

SERVES 6

PISELLI E PATERNOSTRI
Peas and Paternostri

3 pounds fresh peas, unshelled
1 tablespoon unbleached all-purpose flour
  Coarse-grained salt
25 sprigs Italian parsley, leaves only
1 small clove garlic, peeled
½ cup olive oil
1 cup warm beef broth, preferably

homemade
  Salt and freshly ground black pepper
½ pound very short tubular dried pasta,
  such as *paternostri, avemarie* or *ditalini*

TO SERVE
15 sprigs Italian parsley, leaves only

Wash the unshelled peas very well under cold running water. Then shell them and save both the peas and the pods.

Put the peas in a bowl of cold water. Mix the flour into the water and let the peas soak for ½ hour to tenderize them.

Put the pea pods in a large pot of cold water over medium heat, and bring to a boil. Add coarse-grained salt to taste, and cook the pods for 20 minutes. Drain, reserving the cooking water and discarding the pods.

Drain and rinse the peas.

Coarsely chop the parsley and finely chop the garlic on a board.

Heat the oil in a heavy saucepan over medium heat. When the oil is warm, add the chopped ingredients and sauté for 1 minute. Add the peas, cover the pan and cook for 5 minutes. Add ½ cup of the broth and taste for salt and pepper. Cover the pan again and cook over low heat, adding more broth as needed, until the peas are cooked but still firm, about 15 to 25 minutes, depending on the size of the peas.

Meanwhile, return the water in which the pea pods were cooked to a boil.

Add the pasta to the boiling water and stir with a wooden spoon. Cover the pot to bring the water back to a boil as quickly as possible. Then uncover the pot and cook the pasta until it is al dente (9 to 12 minutes, depending on the brand).

Drain the pasta and transfer it to the pan with the peas. Stir very well and cook for 1 minute longer. Taste again for salt and pepper. Serve immediately, sprinkled with the parsley.

SERVES 4 TO 6

MINESTRONE ALLA GENOVESE
Minestrone Genoese-Style with Pesto Sauce

FOR THE MINESTRONE

½ cup dried *cannellini* beans
 Coarse-grained salt
1 leek or 1 large red onion, cleaned
1 medium-sized red onion, cleaned
3 medium-sized celery stalks
15 sprigs Italian parsley, leaves only
1 large boiling potato (not a new potato),
 about 6 ounces
3 medium-sized carrots, scraped
½ cup olive oil
1 ripe tomato, blanched, peeled and seeded
1 cup hot beef broth, preferably homemade
 Salt and freshly ground black pepper

FOR THE PESTO SAUCE

6 whole walnuts, shelled

1 tablespoon pignoli (pine nuts)
1 tablespoon sweet butter
1½ cups loosely packed fresh basil leaves
2 heaping tablespoons drained boiled
 spinach
2 medium-sized cloves garlic, peeled
¾ cup olive oil
2 ounces *parmigiano-reggiano*, freshly grated
2 ounces *pecorino sardo*, freshly grated, or
 2 additional ounces *parmigiano-reggiano*,
 freshly grated
 Salt and freshly ground black pepper

PLUS

½ pound short tubular dried pasta, such as
 elbow macaroni

Soak the beans overnight in a bowl of cold water.

The next morning, bring 10 cups cold water to a boil in a casserole, then add coarse-grained salt to taste. Drain the beans, rinse them under cold running water and add them to the casserole. Simmer, half-covered, until they are cooked but still firm, 45 minutes to 1½ hours, depending on the dryness of the beans. Stir the beans occasionally while they cook.

When the beans are ready, drain them, saving their cooking liquid. Put the beans into a crockery or glass bowl and cover the bowl with aluminum foil.

Meanwhile, clean the leek, if using, removing and discarding the green part. Wash the white part very well. Coarsely chop the leek, onion(s), celery and parsley together on a board.

Peel the potato and cut it into ½-inch pieces.

Cut the carrots lengthwise into quarters. Then cut the quarters into ½-inch pieces.

Heat the oil in a stockpot and add the chopped ingredients, potato and carrots. Sauté for 5 minutes, stirring with a wooden spoon. Add the tomato and sauté for 5 minutes longer. Add the hot broth and cook for 5 minutes. Season with salt and pepper.

Add the cooking liquid from the beans to the stockpot and simmer, uncovered, for ½ hour.

While the minestrone is simmering, prepare the pesto: Put the walnuts, pignoli, butter, basil, spinach, garlic and ¼ cup of the oil in a blender or food processor and grind until very fine. Add the remaining oil and blend all the ingredients together until very smooth. Transfer the ground ingredients to a crockery or glass bowl. Add the *parmigiano-reggiano* and *pecorino sardo* cheese and salt and pepper. Mix all the ingredients together with a wooden spoon. Cover the bowl with aluminum foil and let stand until needed.

Raise the heat under the stockpot and bring the liquid to a boil. Add the pasta and cook until it is al dente (9 to 12 minutes, depending on the brand).

Remove the stockpot from the heat, add the reserved beans and mix very well. Let stand for 2 minutes. Add half of the pesto to the stockpot, stir very well and serve, adding some of the remaining pesto to each serving.

SERVES 8 TO 10

SEDANINI ALLA CRUDAIOLA IN SALSA PICCANTE
Pasta with Savory Uncooked Vegetable Sauce

FOR THE SAUCE

1½ pounds ripe tomatoes
  Coarse-grained salt
2 medium-sized cloves garlic, peeled but left whole
  Juice of ½ lemon
4 medium-sized inner celery stalks, well scraped
2 whole anchovies packed in salt, boned and rinsed, or 4 anchovy fillets packed in oil, drained
3 tablespoons capers in wine vinegar, drained and rinsed under cold water
3 ounces pitted large Greek olives in brine, cut into small pieces

½ cup olive oil
  Salt and freshly ground black pepper

OPTIONAL
½ teaspoon hot red pepper flakes

PLUS
1 pound short tubular dried pasta, such as *sedanini* or *penne*, preferably imported Italian

TO COOK THE PASTA
  Coarse-grained salt

TO SERVE
20 large sprigs Italian parsley, leaves only
15 large fresh basil leaves

Blanch the tomatoes in salted boiling water, then remove the skins and seeds, leaving the tomato fillets whole. Place the tomatoes in a crockery or glass bowl along with the garlic. If using the hot red pepper flakes, season the tomatoes with them. Pour the lemon juice over the tomatoes. Do not mix.

Cut the celery into pieces the same size as the pasta and soak the pieces in a bowl of cold water for ½ hour.

Cut the anchovies into small pieces. Place the anchovies, capers and olives in a bowl. Drain the celery and add it to the bowl. Add the olive oil and season with salt and pepper, but do not mix. Cover the bowl and refrigerate for at least 1 hour, or until needed.

Bring a large pot of cold water to a boil, and add coarse salt to taste.

Add the pasta to the boiling water and cook until al dente (9 to 12 minutes, depending on the brand).

Meanwhile, mix the tomato fillets with the anchovy mixture.

Coarsely chop the parsley.

When the pasta is ready, drain and transfer to a large serving platter. Pour the anchovy sauce over the pasta and combine well. Sprinkle on the parsley and basil. Mix again and serve.

SERVES 4 TO 6

FAGIOLI ED ORZO
Bean-Barley Soup

1 cup pearl barley or farro wheat
1 cup dried *borlotti* (Roman beans) or cranberry or pinto beans
1 medium-sized celery stalk
1 medium-sized carrot, scraped
1 medium-sized red onion, cleaned
4 basil leaves, fresh or preserved in salt (see page 122)
5 sprigs Italian parsley, leaves only
2 large sage leaves, fresh or preserved in salt (see page 122)
3 ounces *pancetta* or prosciutto, in one piece

¾ pound all-purpose potatoes
5 tablespoons olive oil
1 bay leaf
  Coarse-grained salt and freshly ground black pepper
1 to 2 cups chicken broth, preferably homemade, if needed

TO SERVE
Freshly ground black pepper

OPTIONAL
8 to 10 teaspoons olive oil

Soak the barley or farro wheat and the beans separately overnight in bowls of cold water.

The next morning, drain the beans. (Leave the barley in its bowl of water until needed.)

Place 12 cups of cold water and the beans in a heavy medium-sized casserole over medium heat and bring to a simmer.

Meanwhile, coarsely chop the celery, carrot, onion, basil, parsley and sage all together on a board. Cut the *pancetta* or prosciutto into tiny pieces.

Peel the potatoes, cut them into 1-inch squares and put them in a bowl of cold water until needed.

Heat the oil in a medium-sized saucepan over medium heat and, when the oil is warm, add the chopped ingredients along with the *pancetta* and bay leaf. Sauté for 5 minutes, stirring every so often with a wooden spoon.

Add the contents of the saucepan to the casserole containing the beans. Drain the potatoes and add them to the casserole. Cover, lower the heat and sim-

mer for 1 hour.

Remove the bay leaf, then pass the bean mixture through a food mill, using the disc with medium-sized holes, into a large bowl. Then pass the bean mixture through the food mill a second time, using the disc with the smallest holes, back into the casserole. Set the casserole over medium heat. Season the bean mixture with coarse salt and black pepper and simmer for about 10 minutes.

Drain the barley and rinse it under cold running water, then add it to the simmering bean mixture. Cook for about 25 minutes, or until the barley is soft, stirring every so often with a wooden spoon. Taste for salt and pepper.

If the soup is too thick, add chicken broth and bring to a simmer.

The soup may be served hot or at room temperature, with a twist of freshly ground black pepper and, if desired, a teaspoon of olive oil over each serving.

SERVES 8 TO 10

CACCIUCCO CON BATTUTO ALLA LIVORNESE
Fish Soup with Chopped Vegetables Livorno-Style

6 pounds mixed fish and shellfish, cleaned, saving the heads of the fish
1 large lemon
 Coarse-grained salt

FOR THE SAUCE
1 large red onion, cleaned
2 medium-sized celery stalks
2 carrots, scraped
15 sprigs Italian parsley, leaves only
4 large cloves garlic, peeled
15 basil leaves, fresh or preserved in salt (see page 122)
¾ cup olive oil
 Salt and freshly ground black pepper
 A large pinch of hot red pepper flakes
1 cup dry red wine

4 tablespoons tomato paste, preferably imported Italian

FOR THE FISH BROTH
1 carrot, scraped
1 small red onion, cleaned
1 celery stalk
1 clove garlic, peeled
2 quarts lukewarm water
 Coarse-grained salt

TO SERVE
20 sprigs Italian parsley, leaves only
20 fresh basil leaves
8 large slices Tuscan bread or any other crusty saltless bread, lightly toasted and rubbed on both sides with garlic

Cut the fish into 3-inch pieces. If using squid or cuttlefish, cut into rings about ½ inch wide. If using octopus, if large, cut into 2-inch pieces; if very small, leave whole. Place all of the fish and shellfish in a large bowl of cold water with the lemon cut in half and a little coarse salt. Let sit for ½ hour.

Prepare the sauce: Coarsely chop the onion, celery, carrots, parsley, garlic and basil all together on a board.

Heat the olive oil in a large casserole over medium heat and, when the oil is warm, add all of the chopped ingredients. Sauté for 15 minutes, stirring every so often with a wooden spoon. Season with salt and pepper and the hot red pepper flakes. Remove from the heat.

Prepare the fish broth: Cut all of the vegetables into large pieces on a board. Coarsely chop the garlic.

Place the water, vegetables and garlic in a medium-sized stockpot. Add the fish heads and set the pot over medium heat. When the water reaches a boil, add coarse salt to taste and simmer for 45 minutes.

Meanwhile, drain the cleaned fish and rinse it under cold running water. Return the casserole with the sautéed vegetables to medium heat, and add the fish that requires the longest cooking time, such as octopus, calamari and cuttlefish. When they are almost cooked, add the fish with the next longest cooking time, and when those are almost done, add

A Chioggia fisherman selects and aranges the night's catch, dividing sardines from anchovies.

the next ones and so on. In this way none of the fish will be overcooked.

About 4 minutes before the fish are cooked, add the wine and cook for 2 minutes more. Add the tomato paste, mix very well and cook for 2 minutes more. Transfer everything to a large bowl and cover with aluminum foil.

Strain the fish broth into the large casserole, place over high heat and reduce until a rather thick sauce forms, about ½ hour. Taste for seasoning.

When the sauce is ready, return the fish to the casserole and reheat for a few seconds. Then transfer all of the contents of the casserole to a large warmed serving platter, and sprinkle the parsley and basil all over. Place a slice of bread in each soup plate, top with the fish and sauce and serve.

SERVES 8

PASTA AL BRODETTO
Pasta with Scallops in Fish Sauce

FOR THE FISH SAUCE
20 large sprigs Italian parsley
2 medium-sized celery stalks
1 medium-sized carrot, scraped
1 large red onion, cleaned
3 cloves garlic, peeled
½ cup olive oil
½ cup mild red wine vinegar
2 pounds fish heads
1 lemon
Coarse-grained salt
2 pounds ripe tomatoes or 2 pounds drained canned tomatoes, preferably imported Italian

Salt and freshly ground black pepper
¼ to ½ teaspoon hot red pepper flakes
1 pound scallops

PLUS
1 pound short tubular dried pasta, such as *penne* or rigatoni, preferably imported Italian

TO COOK THE PASTA
Coarse-grained salt

TO SERVE
10 sprigs Italian parsley, leaves only

Prepare the sauce: Finely chop the parsley, celery, carrot, onion and garlic all together on a board.

Place a large casserole with the oil over medium heat and, when the oil is warm, add the chopped ingredients. Sauté for 5 minutes, stirring every so often with a wooden spoon. Add the vinegar and simmer for 20 minutes.

Meanwhile, place the fish heads in a bowl of cold water to which you have added a little coarse salt and half of the lemon (squeeze the lemon juice into the water before dropping in the lemon half). Let soak for 15 minutes.

Drain the fish heads and rinse them under cold running water. Add them to the casserole, cover and cook for 20 minutes.

If using fresh tomatoes, cut them into large pieces. Add the fresh or canned tomatoes to the casserole and season with salt and pepper to taste and

the hot red pepper flakes. Cover the casserole again and simmer for 1 hour, adding up to 1 cup cold water if more liquid is needed.

While the sauce cooks, soak the scallops in a bowl of cold water to which you have added coarse salt and the remaining lemon half (squeeze the lemon juice into the water before dropping in the lemon half).

Remove the fish heads from the sauce and discard. Pass the sauce through a food mill, using the disc with the smallest holes, into a crockery or glass bowl. Return the strained sauce to the casserole and reduce over low heat for about 45 minutes, or until reduced to about 2 cups.

Meanwhile, bring a large pot of cold water to a boil, and add coarse salt to taste.

Add the pasta to the boiling water, and cook until just barely al dente (8 to 11 minutes, depending on the brand).

Drain the scallops, rinse them under cold running water and add to the sauce in the casserole.

When the pasta is ready, drain it and add it to the casserole. Mix very well, taste for salt and pepper and cook for about 1 minute more, until the scallops are cooked through and the pasta is just al dente.

Transfer to a large deep serving platter, sprinkle the parsley all over and serve hot.

SERVES 4 TO 6

*Nets are pulled taut by the abundant
catch of sea scallops.*

PASTA ALLE ERBE ALLA NAPOLETANA
Macaroni Cooked in an Herbed Vegetable Sauce

FOR THE SAUCE

2   ounces *pancetta* or prosciutto, in one piece
2   large red onions, cleaned
2   medium-sized celery stalks
2   medium-sized carrots, scraped
1   small clove garlic, peeled
15 sprigs Italian parsley, leaves only
4   large basil leaves, fresh or preserved in salt (see page 122)
4   tablespoons olive oil
1   pound all-purpose potatoes
    Salt and freshly ground black pepper
4   tablespoons tomato paste, preferably

imported Italian
2   to 2½ quarts hot chicken or meat broth, preferably homemade

PLUS

1   pound dried short curly pasta, such as *fusilli* or *tortiglioni*, preferably imported Italian

TO SERVE

    Freshly grated *parmigiano-reggiano*
    Freshly ground black pepper
20 large fresh basil leaves, torn into thirds

Cut the *pancetta* or prosciutto into tiny pieces. Finely chop the onions, celery, carrots, garlic, parsley and basil all together on a board.

Heat the olive oil in a medium-sized stockpot over medium heat and, when the oil is warm, add the *pancetta* or prosciutto. Sauté for 5 minutes. Then add the chopped vegetables and herbs and sauté, stirring every so often with a wooden spoon, until the onions are translucent, about 10 minutes.

Meanwhile, peel the potatoes and thinly slice them.

Add the potato slices to the stockpot. Raise the heat to high, season with salt and pepper and sauté for 5 minutes more.

Dissolve the tomato paste in 2 quarts of the broth. Add the mixture to the stockpot and cook for 20 minutes, or until reduced to 3 to 3½ cups.

Add the pasta to the pot, stir very well and add the remaining hot broth if more liquid is needed in order to cook the pasta. As the pasta cooks, it should absorb the broth, so that when the pasta is almost cooked, after about 10 minutes, there should be no remaining unabsorbed broth. Taste for salt and pepper and let the pasta continue to cook in the sauce, constantly stirring with a wooden spoon, until al dente.

Transfer the contents of the stockpot to a large warmed serving platter and sprinkle on the cheese, followed by the pepper and basil leaves. Serve hot.

SERVES 6 TO 8

RISOTTO AI PEPERONI
Risotto with Sweet Bell Peppers

2 medium-sized sweet yellow bell peppers
2 medium-sized sweet red bell peppers
2 large cloves garlic, peeled
10 large sprigs Italian parsley, leaves only
4 tablespoons olive oil
    About 5 cups boiling chicken or meat broth, preferably homemade
3 cups raw rice, preferably Italian *Arborio*

½ cup dry white wine
    Salt and freshly ground black pepper

TO SERVE
15 sprigs Italian parsley, leaves only
8 tablespoons freshly grated *pecorino romano* or *pecorino sardo*

Clean the yellow peppers, discarding the stems and all the seeds, and cut them into 1-inch pieces. Soak the pieces in a bowl of cold water for ½ hour. Clean the red peppers in the same way and cut them, lengthwise, into ¼-inch strips. Soak the strips in another bowl of cold water for ½ hour.

Finely chop the garlic and coarsely chop the parsley on a board.

Place a heavy casserole with the oil over medium heat and, when the oil is warm, add the chopped ingredients. Sauté for 2 minutes.

Drain the yellow peppers, add them to casserole and cook for 2 or 3 minutes over high heat. Then lower the heat to medium, cover the casserole and cook for about 15 minutes, or until soft, stirring every so often with a wooden spoon and adding a little of the broth if needed.

Pass the contents of the casserole through a food mill, using the disc with smallest holes, into a crockery or glass bowl.

Transfer the pepper purée back to the casserole and set it over medium heat. When the purée starts simmering, add the rice and sauté for 4 minutes, stirring constantly with a wooden spoon. Add the wine and let it evaporate for 2 minutes. Start adding the boiling broth ½ cup at a time, stirring constantly, without adding any additional broth until the previous ½ cup is completely absorbed by the rice. Season with salt and pepper. After 3 cups of the broth have been incorporated, drain the red pepper strips and add them to the casserole. Keep adding broth until the rice is cooked but still al dente; it should be creamy, but still have a "bite" (it will take about 18 minutes from the time the first broth is added).

Remove the risotto from the heat, add the parsley and mix very well. Transfer to a warmed serving platter, sprinkle the cheese all over and serve hot.

SERVES 6 TO 8

SPAGHETTI AL SUGO DI CAVOLFIORE
Spaghetti with Cauliflower Sauce

FOR THE SAUCE
1 medium-sized cauliflower, about 1 ½
   pounds, green leaves removed
3 large cloves garlic, peeled
3 celery stalks
15 sprigs Italian parsley, leaves only
1 medium-sized carrot, scraped
6 tablespoons olive oil
2 tablespoons tomato paste, preferably
   imported Italian
   Salt and freshly ground black pepper
   A large pinch of hot red pepper flakes

2 cups chicken or meat broth, preferably
   homemade

PLUS
1 pound dried spaghetti, preferably imported
   Italian

TO COOK THE PASTA
   Coarse-grained salt

TO SERVE
   Abundant fresh basil and Italian parsley leaves
   Freshly ground black pepper

Soak the cleaned cauliflower in a bowl of cold water for ½ hour.

Meanwhile, coarsely chop the garlic, celery, parsley and carrot all together on a board.

Drain the cauliflower, cut off the florets and discard the stem.

Place a medium-sized casserole with the olive oil over medium heat and, when the oil is warm, add the chopped ingredients. Sauté for 5 minutes. Add the tomato paste, mix very well and season with salt and pepper and the hot red pepper flakes. Add the cauliflower and mix very well. Sauté for 5 minutes, then add ½ cup of the broth and cook, covered, for 15 minutes. Add the remaining broth to the cauliflower, cover again and cook for 15 minutes more. The cauliflower should almost fall apart.

Meanwhile, bring a large pot of cold water to a boil, and add coarse-grained salt to taste.

Add the pasta to the boiling water and cook until just barely al dente (7 to 11 minutes, depending on the brand).

Transfer the contents of the casserole to a large skillet and place the skillet over medium heat. Drain the pasta, transfer to the skillet and mix very well. Cook for 1 minute, mixing constantly with two spoons. At this point the cauliflower should be completely puréed and will coat the pasta. Taste for salt and pepper.

Transfer the pasta to a large serving platter, sprinkle all over with fresh basil and parsley leaves and serve hot, with a twist of black pepper over each serving.

SERVES 4 TO 6

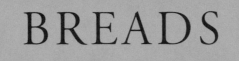

BREADS

PANE DI PRATO
Bread from Prato

FOR THE SPONGE
- 2 cups unbleached all-purpose flour
- 2 ounces (4 cakes) compressed fresh yeast or 4 packages (8 teaspoons) active dry yeast
- 1 cup lukewarm or hot water (depending on the yeast)

FOR THE DOUGH
- 2 cups lukewarm water
- Pinch of salt
- 5 cups unbleached all-purpose flour

Prepare the sponge: Put the flour in a large bowl and make a well in it. Dissolve the yeast in the water. Pour the dissolved yeast into the well and mix with a wooden spoon, incorporating the flour to make a thick batter. Cover the bowl with a cotton dish towel and let rest overnight in a warm place away from drafts.

Prepare the dough: The next morning, add the water a little at a time, stirring continuously with a wooden spoon to dissolve the sponge. Then add the salt and 4 cups of the flour, a small quantity at a time, while stirring with a wooden spoon. Cover the bowl with a cotton dish towel and let rest for ½ hour.

Line the bottom shelf of the oven with unglazed terra-cotta tiles and preheat the oven to 400 degrees.

Spread out the remaining flour on a pasta board and put the risen dough on it. Knead the dough, incorporating more flour. Then divide the dough into 2 pieces and shape them as you wish. Wrap each loaf in a cotton dish towel and let rest for 15 minutes.

Unwrap the loaves and place them directly on the tiles in the oven. Bake for about 1 hour. Remove the loaves from the oven and let them cool on a rack.

MAKES 2 LOAVES

In this small bakery in Sesto Fiorentino, near Florence, bread baking begins at 2 A.M. A baker places loaves on coarse cotton cloth where they are left to rise.

67

SCHIACCIATA CON UVA
Schiacciata with Fresh Grapes

FOR THE SPONGE
1   cup plus 1 tablespoon unbleached all-
    purpose flour
1   ounce (2 cakes) compressed fresh yeast or
    2 packages (4 teaspoons) active dry yeast
¾   cup lukewarm or hot water (depending
    on the yeast)

FOR THE DOUGH
2½ cups unbleached all-purpose flour

2   tablespoons olive oil
    Pinch of salt
    Scant ½ cup lukewarm water

PLUS
2½ pounds red wine grapes (not Concord)
    or 2½ pounds seedless ruby red grapes
1   cup granulated sugar
½   teaspoon fennel seeds

Prepare the sponge: Place the 1 cup of flour in a bowl and make a well in the center. Dissolve the yeast in the water, then pour it into the well. Using a wooden spoon, gradually incorporate the flour into the dissolved yeast. Sprinkle on the remaining tablespoon of flour, cover the bowl with a cotton dish towel and let rest, in a warm place away from drafts, until the sponge has doubled in size, about 1 hour. (Two signs that the sponge has doubled in size are the disappearance of the tablespoon of flour and the formation of large cracks on top.)

Meanwhile, remove the stems from the grapes. Carefully wash the grapes in cold water. Then pat them dry with paper towels and put them in a large crockery or glass bowl. Add the sugar and fennel seeds. Mix with a wooden spoon so that the grapes are well coated with the sugar. Let stand until needed.

Prepare the dough: Arrange the flour in a mound on a pasta board and make a well in the flour. Pour the sponge into the well along with the olive oil, salt and water. Use a wooden spoon to mix together all the ingredients in the well. Then start mixing with your hands, incorporating the flour, little by little,

from the inside rim of the well. Keep mixing until all but about 5 tablespoons of the flour are incorporated. Then knead the dough with the palm of your hand, incorporating the remaining flour in a folding motion, until the dough is homogeneous and smooth, about 2 minutes.

Oil a 14-inch pizza pan.

Divide the dough in half. With a rolling pin, roll out both pieces into rounds about 16 inches in diameter. Lay one piece on the bottom of the oiled pan. Distribute half of the sugared grapes over the layer of dough, cover with the other layer of dough and seal the two edges together all around by pressing them together.

Distribute the remaining grapes on top of the *schiacciata,* cover the pan with a cotton dish towel and let rest until the *schiacciata* has risen to almost double in size, about 1 hour.

Preheat the oven to 375 degrees.

When the dough has doubled in size, remove the towel and bake the *schiacciata* for 1 hour. Remove from the oven and let cool completely, about 1 hour. Serve from the pan or on a board to preserve its rustic character, slicing it like a pizza.

FOCACCIA AL BASILICO
Focaccia with Basil

FOR THE SPONGE
2 cups plus 1 tablespoon unbleached all-purpose flour
½ ounce compressed fresh yeast or 1 package (2 teaspoons) active dry yeast
1 cup lukewarm or hot water (depending on the yeast)
   Pinch of salt

FOR THE DOUGH
1¼ cups unbleached all-purpose flour
4 tablespoons (2 ounces) sweet butter or lard, at room temperature

¼ cup lukewarm water
   Salt and freshly ground black pepper

PLUS
6 tablespoons olive oil
15 large fresh basil leaves
   Coarse-grained salt

TO SERVE
   Olive oil
   Coarse-grained salt
20 fresh basil leaves

Prepare the sponge: Place the 2 cups of flour in a large bowl and make a well in the center. Dissolve the yeast in the water, then pour it into the well along with the salt. Use a wooden spoon to gradually incorporate the flour. Sprinkle on the remaining tablespoon of flour, cover the bowl with a cotton dish towel and let rest, in a warm place away from drafts, until the sponge has doubled in size, about 1 hour. (Two signs that the sponge has doubled in size are the disappearance of the tablespoon of flour and the formation of large cracks on top.)

Prepare the dough: When the sponge is ready, spread out the flour on a board and place the sponge on it. Add the butter or lard, water and salt and pepper, and start incorporating all the ingredients into the sponge, kneading in a folding motion, until all the flour is incorporated and the dough is elastic and smooth.

Use 2 tablespoons of the oil to grease a 15½-by-10½-inch jelly-roll pan.

Use a rolling pin to stretch the dough to the same size as the jelly-roll pan, then place the dough in the pan, spreading it out to reach the sides, if necessary. Use your index finger to make 15 indentations all over the top of the dough. Place a basil leaf in each one, then sprinkle coarse salt all over and drip the remaining 4 tablespoons olive oil over to cover the entire surface. Prick the dough all over with a fork, then cover the pan with a piece of plastic wrap. Place a cotton dish towel over the pan and let the dough rest, in a warm place away from drafts, until doubled in size, about 1 hour.

Preheat the oven to 400 degrees.

When the dough is ready, remove the towel, the plastic wrap and the basil leaves, and bake for 35 minutes. Remove from the oven and cut into squares. Serve hot with more olive oil and coarse salt and the fresh basil leaves.

SERVES 12

GRISSINI AL RAMERINO
Rosemary Grissini

FOR THE SPONGE

2 cups plus 1 tablespoon unbleached all-purpose flour

½ ounce compressed fresh yeast or 1 package (2 teaspoons) active dry yeast

1½ cups lukewarm or hot water (depending on the yeast)

½ teaspoon salt

FOR THE DOUGH

2½ cups unbleached all-purpose flour

4 tablespoons olive oil

4 tablespoons rosemary leaves, fresh or preserved in salt or dried and blanched (see page 122), very coarsely chopped
Salt and freshly ground black pepper

Prepare the sponge: Place the 2 cups of flour in a large bowl and make a well in the center. Dissolve the yeast in the water, then pour it into the well along with the salt. Use a wooden spoon to gradually incorporate the flour, little by little. Sprinkle on the remaining tablespoon of flour, cover the bowl with a cotton dish towel and let rest, in a warm place away from drafts, until the sponge has doubled in size, about 1 hour. (Two signs that the sponge has doubled in size are the disappearance of the tablespoon of flour and the formation of large cracks on top.)

Prepare the dough: Spread 2 cups of the flour on a board and place the sponge on it. Make a well in the sponge, then add the olive oil, along with the rosemary and salt and pepper to taste. First incorporate the oil and the rosemary into the sponge, then, little by little, incorporate the flour, until a ball of dough is formed. Sprinkle the remaining ½ cup of flour on the board and continue kneading the dough

until the flour is incorporated.

Divide the dough into 4 pieces. Pass each piece through a pasta machine, set at its widest setting, three or four times. Then fold each piece in half and press so that the two layers stick together well.

Insert the *tagliatelle* cutter on the pasta machine. Pass each piece of dough through the cutter, immediately peeling off each individual strip by hand, as the machine cuts them but does not separate them completely. Transfer the strips of dough to floured cookie sheets, being careful to place them far enough apart to keep them from sticking to each other once risen. When all the pieces of dough have been cut, cover the cookie sheets with cotton towels and let the *grissini* rest, in a warm place away from drafts, until doubled in size, about 1 hour.

Preheat the oven to 375 degrees.

When ready, bake the *grissini* for ½ hour, or until very crisp and golden.

MAKES ABOUT 40

MAIN COURSES

SOGLIOLE IN SAOR
Marinated Fried Sole Venetian-Style

2 pounds small sole or flounder fillets
4 extra-large eggs
  Pinch of salt
¼ cup cold milk

FOR THE SAUCE
1 large white onion, cleaned
½ cup olive oil
4 tablespoons (2 ounces) sweet butter
10 black peppercorns
5 bay leaves
½ cup white wine vinegar

1 cup cold water
  Salt and freshly ground black pepper

PLUS
15 sprigs Italian parsley, leaves only
2 medium-sized cloves garlic, peeled
¼ cup raisins
4 cups vegetable oil
4 tablespoons (2 ounces) sweet butter
1 cup unseasoned bread crumbs, preferably homemade, lightly toasted
2 tablespoons pignoli (pine nuts)

Cut the fillets into pieces not larger than 2 by 4 inches.

With a fork, lightly beat the eggs, salt and the milk in a bowl. Add the fish pieces to the bowl, mix very well and let the fish marinate for 1 hour, mixing occasionally.

Meanwhile, prepare the sauce: Cut the onion into very thin rings and place in a bowl of cold water to soak for 5 minutes.

Heat the oil and butter in a heavy saucepan over medium heat. When the butter is completely melted, drain the onion rings and add them to the pan. Sauté over low heat for 5 minutes, or until the onion rings are translucent. Add the peppercorns, bay leaves and wine vinegar to the pan. Cook slowly for 2 minutes. Then add the water and simmer for ½ hour. Season with salt and pepper to taste. Keep the sauce warm while cooking the fish.

Finely chop the parsley and garlic together on a board. Soak the raisins in a bowl of lukewarm water for 15 minutes.

When the fish has marinated for an hour, heat the vegetable oil with the butter in a deep-fat fryer. Lay a sheet of aluminum foil on a board and spread the bread crumbs on the foil. Remove the fish pieces, one at a time, from the egg mixture, and bread them on both sides, pressing the fish pieces all over with the palm of your hand to make sure that both sides are coated uniformly.

When the oil is hot (about 375 degrees), add the fish pieces and cook for 1 minute on each side. Transfer the cooked fish to a large serving platter (do not line the platter with paper towels). When all the fish pieces are cooked, sprinkle them with the chopped ingredients.

Drain the raisins, pat them dry with paper towels and spread them all over the fish, along with the pignoli. Pour the hot sauce over everything. Cover the platter with aluminum foil and let stand for at least 1 hour before serving.

SERVES 6

INVOLTINI DI PESCE SPADA
Rolled Stuffed Swordfish Cutlets on Skewers

3 pounds swordfish with bone, cut into three ½-inch-thick slices
4 tablespoons olive oil
  Salt

FOR THE STUFFING
2 medium-sized cloves garlic, peeled
3 heaping tablespoons capers in wine vinegar, drained
½ cup very fine unseasoned bread crumbs, preferably homemade, lightly toasted

Juice of ½ lemon
Salt and freshly ground black pepper

PLUS
2 lemons
3 large ripe but not overripe tomatoes
  Salt and freshly ground black pepper

TO SERVE
  Lemon wedges
18 sprigs Italian parsley, leaves only

78

Cut each slice of fish crosswise into 2 pieces, removing the bone in the center. Put the 6 pieces of fish in a bowl and add the olive oil. Sprinkle salt over the fish and let it stand for ½ hour, turning the pieces over two or three times.

Prepare the stuffing: Finely chop the garlic and coarsely chop the capers on a board. Put the chopped ingredients in a small bowl and add the bread crumbs, lemon juice and salt and pepper to taste. Mix all the ingredients together with a wooden spoon.

Preheat the oven to 375 degrees.

Remove the fish slices from the bowl and lay them on a platter. Place one sixth of the stuffing in the center of each slice.

Cut the lemons and tomatoes into ½-inch-thick slices.

Thread a long skewer, starting with a slice of tomato, then of lemon, and then a slice of the fish folded like a package. Repeat until all the ingredients are used. Brush everything threaded on the skewer with the oil left in the bowl and then sprinkle with salt and pepper.

Put the skewer on a jelly-roll pan or baking sheet and put it on the middle shelf of the oven. Bake for 20 minutes. Then raise the temperature to 500 degrees and cook for 3 minutes longer. Remove the skewer from the oven and transfer it to a serving platter. Serve with the lemon wedges and parsley leaves.

SERVES 6

CANESTRELLI DI CHIOGGIA
Scallops Chioggia-Style

18 sea scallops, about 1½ pounds
½ tablepoon coarse-grained salt
2 medium-sized cloves garlic, peeled
10 sprigs Italian parsley, leaves only
⅓ cup olive oil
   Salt and freshly ground black pepper
¼ cup dry white wine

2 tablespoons brandy
   Juice of 1 lemon

PLUS
   Scallop shells, for serving
15 sprigs Italian parsley, leaves only, finely chopped
1 lemon, cut into slices

Put the scallops into a bowl of cold water and add the coarse-grained salt. Let the scallops soak for ½ hour.

Finely chop the garlic and the parsley leaves together on a board.

Drain the scallops and pat them dry with paper towels.

Heat the oil in a frying pan over medium heat. When the oil is warm, add the chopped ingredients and sauté for 2 minutes. Then add the scallops, lower the heat, cover the pan and cook for 5 minutes. Season with salt and pepper. Add the wine and let it evaporate for 5 minutes. Then add the brandy and cook for 5 minutes longer, or until evaporated.

Heat the scallop shells in the oven for a few minutes.

When the brandy has evaporated, add the lemon juice and mix it in very well. Transfer the scallops to the heated scallop shells and serve immediately, with the chopped parsley leaves and lemon slices.

SERVES 3 AS A MAIN COURSE OR 6 AS AN APPETIZER

CARPACCIO
Carpaccio

1 medium-sized clove garlic, peeled but left whole
½ cup olive oil
Juice of 3 lemons
Salt and freshly ground black pepper

1 pound white mushrooms
8 *scaglie* (thin slices *parmigiano-reggiano*: about 2 ounces each)
8 very thin slices beef top round
8 sprigs Italian parsley, leaves only

Hold the garlic with a fork and rub it over the entire inside surface of a medium-sized crockery or glass bowl, using a rotating motion. Then, using your other hand, slowly drip in all of the olive oil, while continuing to rotate the fork with the garlic and using it to whip up the oil, about 3 minutes.

Add the lemon juice in the same way, using the rotating fork to mix it thoroughly with the oil, about 2 minutes longer. To this very light emulsion, add salt and pepper to taste. Let the sauce stand until needed.

Remove any soil clinging to the mushrooms with a damp paper towel, then thinly slice them and arrange them in the center of a crockery or china platter. Make an outer ring of the *parmigiano-reggiano* slices over the mushrooms, then lay the meat in the center, inside the ring of cheese. Pour the prepared sauce over everything. Arrange the parsley on the platter and serve.

The dish may be prepared in advance and kept covered in the refrigerator, but the color of the meat and the mushrooms will darken.

SERVES 8

81

OSSOBUCO ALLE VERDURE
Ossobuco in a Vegetable Sauce

FOR THE OSSOBUCO

2   medium-sized zucchini, ends trimmed
2   medium-sized carrots, scraped
1   medium-sized red onion, cleaned
1   medium-sized celery stalk
20 sprigs Italian parsley, leaves only
6   *ossibuchi* (veal shank cut into 1½-inch slices, with bone and marrow)
½   cup unbleached all-purpose flour
6   tablespoons (3 ounces) sweet butter
2   tablespoons olive oil
2   tablespoons tomato paste, preferably imported Italian
¼   cup lukewarm chicken or beef broth, preferably homemade
2   cups dry white wine

Salt and freshly ground black pepper
1   teaspoon dried thyme

FOR THE VEGETABLES

¾   pound fresh peas, shelled
¾   pound string beans
¾   pound carrots, scraped
¾   pound celery hearts
    Coarse-grained salt

PLUS

6   tablespoons (3 ounces) sweet butter
2   tablespoons olive oil
    Salt and freshly ground black pepper
    Pinch of freshly grated nutmeg

Cut the zucchini, carrots, onion and celery into small pieces and put them in a bowl of cold water along with the parsley. Let soak until needed.

Tie each ossobuco with string to keep it together while it cooks. Lightly flour the *ossibuchi* on both sides with the ½ cup flour.

Heat the butter and oil in a casserole over medium heat and, when the butter is completely melted, add the meat. Sauté until it is golden brown on both sides, about 3 minutes on each side.

Dissolve the tomato paste in the broth, add it to the casserole and cook for 2 minutes. Add ½ cup of the wine to the casserole and let it evaporate for 10 minutes.

Drain the chopped vegetables and add them to the casserole. Cover and cook over medium heat for 20 minutes. Taste for salt and pepper. Turn the *ossi-buchi* over and add the remaining 1½ cups of wine and the thyme. Cover the casserole again and cook for at least 35 minutes longer, or until the meat is very tender.

Meanwhile, prepare the vegetables: Fill four bowls with cold water. Put the peas in one and let them soak for ½ hour. As each of the other vegetables is cleaned, put it in its own bowl to soak for the same length of time.

Clean the string beans, removing the ends.

Cut the carrots into quarters lengthwise. Then cut each quarter into 2-inch pieces.

Remove the strings from the celery and cut each stalk into 3 long strips. Then cut each strip into 2-inch pieces.

Bring four small pots of cold water to a boil; then add coarse-grained salt. Place each vegetable in its own pot and boil each one until it is cooked but still firm, about 15 minutes. Drain the vegetables and let them stand until needed.

When the meat is tender, taste for salt and pepper and transfer the meat to a serving platter. Cover the platter to keep the *ossibuchi* warm.

Pass the remaining contents of the casserole through a food mill, using the disc with the smallest holes, into a large bowl. Return the passed ingredients to the casserole and cook over medium heat for 15 minutes, or until a thick, smooth sauce is formed.

Meanwhile, heat the butter and oil in a saucepan. When the butter is completely melted, add the boiled vegetables and season them with salt and pepper and the nutmeg. Sauté gently for 5 minutes.

Return the meat to the casserole with the reduced sauce to reheat and to absorb some of the sauce.

Remove the strings from the *ossibuchi*. Arrange an ossobuco, some of the sauce and some of the sautéed vegetables on each plate.

SERVES 6

SALSICCIA DI POLLO E VITELLA AL PEPE VERDE
Chicken and Veal Galantine-Sausage with Green Peppercorns

1 chicken, about 3½ pounds
¼ pound prosciutto, sliced very thin
¾ pound ground veal
1 cup heavy cream
 Salt and freshly ground black pepper
1 tablespoon green peppercorns preserved in brine, drained
1 teaspoon olive oil

FOR THE SAUCE
3 tablespoons green peppercorns preserved in brine, drained

4 tablespoons olive oil
 Salt and freshly ground black pepper
1 medium-sized clove garlic, peeled
2 tablespoons (1 ounce) sweet butter, at room temperature
1 scant tablespoon unbleached all-purpose flour
¾ cup lukewarm chicken broth, preferably homemade
1 tablespoon freshly squeezed lemon juice
1 scant tablespoon red wine vinegar

Cut through the two tendons at the end of each of the two chicken legs. Cut the skin of the chicken lengthwise down the back and, using a paring knife, carefully remove the entire skin in one piece. Spread out the skin on a board with the inside of the skin facing up. Cover the skin completely with the prosciutto slices.

Remove the skinned breast from the chicken and coarsely grind it in a meat grinder into a crockery or glass bowl. Save the rest of the chicken for later use. Add the ground veal and then the heavy cream. Season with salt and pepper to taste. Mix all the ingredients together very well with a wooden spoon.

Rinse the peppercorns in cold water and add them to the bowl. Mix again to incorporate the peppercorns with the other ingredients. Transfer the stuffing onto one end of the prepared chicken skin, and roll it up like a salami.

Oil the shiny side of a large piece of aluminum foil with the olive oil and place the chicken galantine on the foil. Wrap it like a package and refrigerate it for ½ hour.

Preheat the oven to 375 degrees.

Bake the wrapped galantine-sausage in a baking dish for 1 hour, turning the package once. Remove from the oven and let rest, wrapped, for ½ hour.

Prepare the sauce: Finely chop the peppercorns on a board and transfer them to a small crockery or glass bowl. Add the oil and salt and pepper to taste. Mix all the ingredients well with a wooden spoon. Let stand until needed.

Finely chop the garlic and transfer it to a second crockery or glass bowl. Add the butter and flour to the garlic and combine all the ingredients with a fork until a thick paste is formed. Then add the broth, lemon juice and wine vinegar and mix again with a wooden spoon, adding a pinch of salt and pepper.

Transfer the contents of the first bowl to a small heavy saucepan and place it over low heat. Sauté gently for 5 minutes, stirring occasionally with a wooden spoon. Then add the contents of the second bowl and mix very well to be sure that no lumps form. Simmer for about 10 minutes, until a smooth sauce has formed.

When the sauce is ready, unwrap the meat and cut it into 6 slices. For each serving, place a slice of the galantine-sausage on one side of a plate and spoon the sauce onto the other side of the plate (not over the meat). Serve immediately.

SERVES 6

POLLO AI LIMONI
Chicken Roasted with Lemon Halves

1 chicken, about 3½ pounds
4 lemons
2 medium-sized cloves garlic, peeled
15 sprigs Italian parsley, leaves only

Salt and freshly ground black pepper
½ teaspoon hot red pepper flakes

TO SERVE
Sprigs of Italian parsley

Clean the chicken, removing the excess fat from the cavity. Open the chicken up by cutting it lengthwise through the breast bone (not down the back). Put the flattened bird in a large crockery or glass bowl. Squeeze the lemons and pour the juice over the chicken. Add the lemon halves to the bowl.

Finely chop the garlic and parsley together on a board and add them to the bowl, with salt and pepper to taste and the hot red pepper flakes. Let the chicken marinate for 1 hour in a cool place or on the bottom shelf of the refrigerator, turning it four times.

Preheat the oven to 400 degrees.

Transfer the chicken to a baking dish, preferably of terra-cotta, and pour the marinade from the bowl over it. Arrange the lemon halves on the chicken and roast for 45 minutes.

Remove the chicken from the oven and serve immediately, with a few sprigs of parsley.

SERVES 4

86

POLLO AI PEPERONI AL FORNO
Chicken Baked with Peppers

3 large sweet red bell peppers
3 large sweet yellow peppers
3 whole anchovies packed in salt, boned and rinsed, or 6 anchovy fillets, packed in oil, drained
3 large cloves garlic, peeled
4 ounces *pancetta* or prosciutto, in one piece
¾ cup olive oil
1½ tablespoons red wine vinegar

Salt and freshly ground black pepper

OPTIONAL
1 teaspoon hot red pepper flakes

PLUS
1 chicken, about 3½ pounds

TO SERVE
20 sprigs Italian parsley, leaves only, coarsely chopped

Singe the skin of the peppers by roasting them on hot ash, or by steaming them on the middle shelf of a 375-degree oven with a baking pan full of water on the bottom shelf. Remove the skin, seeds and stems under cold running water, then cut the peppers into 1-inch strips. Let rest until needed.

Preheat the oven to 400 degrees.

Finely chop the anchovies along with the garlic on a board. Transfer to a crockery or glass bowl.

Cut the *pancetta* or prosciutto into tiny pieces and add to the bowl with the anchovy mixture. Add the olive oil, vinegar and salt and pepper to taste, plus the red hot pepper flakes (if using), and mix everything together with a wooden spoon.

Clean and carefully wash the chicken, then cut it into 8 pieces.

Lightly oil a 13½-by-8¾-inch baking dish. Cover the bottom of the dish with half of the peppers, pour half of the anchovy mixture over them and arrange the chicken pieces on top. Distribute the remaining peppers over the chicken, then the remaining anchovy mixture. Cover the dish with aluminum foil and bake for 1 hour, or until the chicken is cooked and the peppers have almost dissolved to form a thick sauce.

Transfer the chicken to a warm serving dish. Stir the peppers very well with a wooden spoon, then pour the sauce over the bird. Sprinkle with the parsley and serve hot.

The classic way to serve this chicken dish is with slices of bread, toasted and lightly rubbed with garlic.

SERVES 4 TO 6

STRACOTTO DI VITELLA ALLA FORNARINA
Roasted Veal Shank

FOR THE *STRACOTTO*

3   pounds boneless veal shank, cut into 2-inch cubes
2   tablespoons unbleached all-purpose flour
6   tablespoons olive oil
3   large cloves garlic, peeled but left whole
5   large sage leaves, fresh or preserved in salt (see page 122)
1   tablespoon rosemary leaves, fresh or preserved in salt or dried and blanched (see page 122)
2   pounds very ripe tomatoes, cut into pieces, or 2 pounds drained canned tomatoes, preferably imported Italian
2   tablespoons tomato paste, preferably imported Italian
1   cup dry red wine

Salt and freshly ground black pepper
A large pinch of hot red pepper flakes
1   to 2 cups chicken or meat broth, preferably homemade, if needed

TO SERVE

Coarse-grained salt
4   pounds spinach
2   medium-sized cloves garlic, peeled
5   tablespoons olive oil
Salt and freshly ground black pepper
A large pinch of hot red pepper flakes

PLUS

6   slices Tuscan bread or any other crusty, saltless bread, ½ inch thick, lightly toasted and rubbed with garlic

Lightly flour the meat by placing it in a colander, sprinkling the flour over it and shaking the colander to remove the excess flour.

Heat the oil in a medium-sized casserole over medium heat and, when the oil is warm, add the garlic, sage and rosemary. Sauté, stirring with a wooden spoon, for 5 minutes, or until the garlic is golden.

Strain the oil, discarding the sautéed garlic and aromatic herbs. Pour the oil back into the casserole, set it over low heat and add the veal. Sauté for 5 minutes, stirring every so often with a wooden spoon.

Meanwhile, pass the fresh or canned tomatoes through a food mill, using the disc with the smallest holes, into a crockery or glass bowl. Dissolve the tomato paste in the strained tomatoes.

Preheat the oven to 375 degrees.

Add the wine to the casserole and let it evaporate for 10 minutes.

Season the meat with salt and pepper and the hot red pepper flakes. Add the tomatoes to the casserole, cover and bake for 1½ hours, adding broth as needed. (It is possible that the meat will give off enough liquid and no broth will be needed.) The meat should be soft and very juicy.

Meanwhile, bring a large pot of cold water to a boil, and add coarse salt to taste. Add the spinach to the pot and boil for 5 minutes.

Drain the spinach and cool under cold running water. Squeeze the spinach dry and coarsely chop it on a board.

Finely chop the garlic.

Heat the oil in a skillet. Add the garlic and sauté

for 20 seconds. Add the spinach, season with salt and pepper and the hot red pepper flakes and sauté for 5 minutes. Keep warm.

When the meat is ready, use a slotted spoon to transfer it to a large serving platter.

Reduce the remaining sauce in the casserole over medium heat until rather thick. Taste for salt and pepper. Pour the sauce over the meat. Arrange the warm spinach all around the meat and serve hot, along with the toasted bread.

SERVES 6

A serving of Stracotto di vitella alla fornarina *(Roasted Veal Shank) and a plate of Tuscan bread rubbed with garlic in front of an abandoned church in the tiny village of Bugialla. My family has always believed that our ancestors lived here many centuries ago as we are the only family with this name.*

SPIEDINI DI GAMBERI IN SALSA
Shrimp on Skewers with Thyme Sauce

FOR THE SHRIMP
18 large or 12 jumbo shrimp
   Coarse-grained salt
1 large lemon
6 to 8 large sprigs fresh rosemary
4 tablespoons olive oil
   Salt and freshly ground black pepper
   Approximately 1 cup, very fine unseasoned bread crumbs, preferably homemade, lightly toasted

FOR THE SAUCE
1 celery stalk
1 medium-sized red onion, cleaned
10 sprigs Italian parsley, leaves only
1 medium-sized carrot, scraped

5 tablespoons (2½ ounces) sweet butter
4 tablespoons olive oil
   Salt and freshly ground black pepper
   A large pinch of freshly grated nutmeg
   A large pinch of ground cinnamon
1 whole clove
½ teaspoon dried thyme
½ cup dry white wine
3 tablespoons unbleached all-purpose flour
2½ cups very hot chicken or meat broth,
   preferably homemade

TO SERVE
2 large very ripe tomatoes, seeded and cut
   into very small pieces
   Sprigs of fresh rosemary

Place the shrimp in a bowl of cold water with coarse salt and the lemon cut in half and squeezed, and soak for ½ hour.

Meanwhile, prepare the sauce: Finely chop the celery, onion, parsley and carrot all together on a board.

Place a saucepan with 2 tablespoons of the butter and the olive oil over medium heat and, when the butter is melted, add the chopped ingredients. Lower the heat to the minimum and sauté as long as possible without burning, stirring every so often with a wooden spoon. Season with salt and pepper, the nutmeg and cinnamon, and add the whole clove along with the thyme. Add the wine and, still over low heat, let all the liquid evaporate; the result should look like a vegetable paste. Remove from the heat and discard the whole clove.

Heat the remaining 3 tablespoons butter in a medium-sized saucepan over medium heat. When the butter is melted, add the flour, mix very well and sauté for 2 minutes. Bring the broth to a boil, add it to the flour mixture and stir very well with a wooden spoon. When the sauce starts simmering, lower the heat to the minimum, and add the vegetable sauce. Simmer for 20 minutes, stirring every so often with a wooden spoon. Remove the sauce from the heat and let rest, covered, until needed.

Prepare the shrimp: Shell and devein the shrimp. Remove all but the top leaves from the sprigs of rosemary. Thread the shrimp onto the rosemary sprigs, bending each shrimp in half to make the letter "C" and passing the rosemary sprig through both halves.

Preheat the oven to 400 degrees.

Place a large skillet with the oil over low heat.

When the oil is warm, add the shrimp *spiedini*, raise the heat to medium, season the shrimp with salt and pepper and sauté for 30 seconds on each side. Season again with salt and pepper.

Spread the bread crumbs on a board, transfer the *spiedini* onto the board and coat them with the crumbs. Place the shrimp, still on the rosemary stems, in a baking dish and bake for about 10 minutes (if jumbo shrimp are used, the baking time will be at least 5 minutes longer).

Meanwhile, reheat the sauce.

Transfer the *spiedini* onto individual plates, ladle some of the sauce and some of the tomato pieces on the side and serve with fresh rosemary sprigs.

SERVES 4 TO 6

POLENTA TARAGNA CON SPEZZATINO DI MAIALE
Cornmeal-Buckwheat Polenta with Pork Stew

FOR THE *SPEZZATINO* (see Note)

2 ounces dried *porcini* mushrooms

4 cups lukewarm water

3 ounces *pancetta* or prosciutto, in one piece

2 tablespoons (1 ounce) sweet butter

2 tablespoons olive oil

2 medium-sized carrots, scraped

1 medium-sized red onion, cleaned

2 medium-sized celery stalks

1 clove garlic, peeled

10 sprigs Italian parsley, leaves only

½ tablespoon rosemary leaves, fresh or preserved in salt or dried and blanched (see page 122)

5 large sage leaves, fresh or preserved in salt (see page 122)

4 pounds boneless pork, from the loin, cut into 2-inch cubes

About 1 cup unbleached all-purpose flour

1½ pounds very ripe tomatoes or 1½ pounds drained canned tomatoes, preferably imported Italian

¾ cup dry red wine

Salt and freshly ground black pepper

FOR THE POLENTA

½ pound coarsely ground yellow Italian cornmeal

½ pound medium-ground buckwheat flour

2½ quarts chicken or meat broth, preferably homemade

8 tablespoons (4 ounces) sweet butter

Salt and freshly ground black pepper

TO SERVE

Sprigs of fresh rosemary and sage

Prepare the *spezzatino*: Soak the mushrooms in the lukewarm water for ½ hour.

Strain the mushrooms, saving the soaking water. Clean the mushrooms very well, being sure no sand remains attached to the stems. Pour the mushroom water through a strainer lined with paper toweling. Repeat this until the water is clear of sand.

Use a meat grinder to coarsely grind the *pancetta* or prosciutto directly into a heavy medium-sized casserole. Add the butter and oil, place the casserole over low heat and lightly sauté the *pancetta* or prosciutto for 5 minutes, stirring every so often with a wooden spoon.

Meanwhile, finely chop the carrots, onion, celery, garlic, parsley, rosemary and sage all together on a board.

Add the chopped ingredients to the casserole and sauté for 10 minutes more.

Place the pork in a large colander, sprinkle the flour over the meat, then shake the colander in order to remove excess flour. In this way the meat will be floured very lightly. Add the floured meat to the vegetables and sauté over medium heat until very lightly golden, about 10 minutes.

While the pork cooks, if using fresh tomatoes, cut them into pieces. Pass the fresh or canned tomatoes through a food mill, using the disc with the smallest holes, into a crockery or glass bowl.

When the meat is ready, add the wine to the casserole and let it evaporate for 5 minutes, stirring every so often with a wooden spoon. Add the mushrooms, mix very well, then add the tomatoes. Season with salt and pepper. Cover the casserole and cook for about ½ hour, stirring every so often with a wooden spoon and adding some of the reserved mushroom water as needed.

Meanwhile, prepare the polenta: Combine the cornmeal and buckwheat flour.

Bring the broth to a boil in a large stockpot over medium heat, then start adding the cornmeal-buckwheat mixture in a slow steady stream, continuously stirring with a large spoon until completely incorporated. Then keep stirring, over medium heat, for 45 minutes more. Two minutes before the polenta is ready, add the butter and taste for salt and pepper.

When the polenta and the meat are ready, use a ladle to transfer, in alternating layers, the polenta and half of the sauce from the meat to a large tureen, finishing with a layer of sauce. Each serving should consist of some of the polenta and sauce from the tureen plus the *spezzatino*, and more sauce on the side. Top each serving with sprigs of fresh rosemary and sage. Serve hot.

SERVES 8 TO 10

Note: *Spezzatino* is a stew made with cubes of meat
or fowl (with bone) cut into small pieces.

AGNELLO ALLE ERBE
Lamb with Herbed Horseradish Sauce

FOR THE LAMB
2 medium-sized cloves garlic, peeled
1 heaping tablespoon rosemary leaves,
  fresh or preserved in salt (see page 122)
5 large basil leaves, fresh or preserved in
  salt (see page 122)
5 large sage leaves, fresh or preserved in
  salt (see page 122)
15 fresh chives
6 tablespoons olive oil
  Salt and freshly ground black pepper

6 large bay leaves
6 loin lamb chops, no thicker than 1 ½
  inches

FOR THE HORSERADISH SAUCE
3 tablespoons grated fresh horseradish
6 tablespoons olive oil

TO SERVE
  Fresh rosemary sprigs
  Fresh sage leaves

Using a mortar and pestle or a blender or food processor, finely grind together the garlic, rosemary, basil, sage and chives. Transfer to a crockery or glass bowl, add the oil and season with salt and pepper. Mix well, then add the bay leaves.

Place the lamb chops on a serving dish, pour all of the marinade over them, cover the dish and let rest in the refrigerator for at least 2 hours.

Prepare the sauce: Place the horseradish in a glass bowl, add the oil and mix very well. Cover the sauce and let rest in the refrigerator until needed.

Set an iron skillet over medium heat. When it is very hot (about 400 degrees), put in the meat and pour all the marinade over it. Cover and cook for 3 minutes for rare and 4 minutes for medium-rare. Turn the meat over, season with salt and pepper and cook, covered, for 1 minute or so, depending on the thickness of the meat.

Serve hot with the sauce from the skillet over each chop and a little horseradish sauce on the side. Arrange rosemary sprigs and sage leaves on top.

SERVES 6

VEGETABLES

BISTECCHE DI MELANZANE
Eggplant Steaks

3 medium-sized eggplants (about 2
   pounds total weight)
   Juice of 2 large lemons
6 tablespoons olive oil
2 large cloves garlic, peeled but left whole
1 teaspoon dried oregano
   Salt and freshly ground black pepper

PLUS
1 cup very fine unseasoned bread crumbs,
   preferably homemade, lightly toasted
   Salt and freshly ground black pepper
2 tablespoons olive oil

TO SERVE
   Lemon wedges

Cut off and discard the stems of the eggplants, then cut them lengthwise into ½-inch slices. Discard the two outer slices of each eggplant that have skin on one side.

Place the eggplant slices in a crockery or glass bowl large enough to hold them in no more than three layers.

Strain the lemon juice into a glass bowl. Add the olive oil, garlic, oregano and salt and pepper to taste. Mix well with a wooden spoon, then pour this mixture over the eggplant slices. Cover the bowl with plastic wrap and marinate in the refrigerator for at least 1 hour, turning the slices at least four times.

Preheat the oven to 400 degrees.

Mix the bread crumbs with salt and pepper to taste and put them on a large serving platter. Heavily oil two baking dishes with the olive oil.

Coat both sides of each eggplant slice with the bread crumbs, firmly pressing the crumbs into the eggplant with the palm of your hand. Arrange the prepared slices in one layer in the oiled baking dishes. Discard the cloves of garlic from the marinade, then pour the marinade over the eggplant. Bake for about 25 minutes. The eggplant should be very soft and a very crisp "crust" of bread crumbs should have formed.

Serve hot, with lemon wedges.

SERVES 6 TO 8

CARCIOFI E PISELLI ALLA ROMANA
Artichokes with Peas Roman-Style

3 large artichokes
1 lemon
½ pound shelled fresh peas or ½ pound frozen petite peas
1 tablespoon unbleached all-purpose flour
3 ounces *pancetta* or prosciutto, in one piece

2 large cloves garlic, peeled
4 tablespoons olive oil
Approximately 1½ cups lukewarm meat or chicken broth, preferably, homemade
Salt and freshly ground black pepper
15 sprigs Italian parsley, leaves only, coarsely chopped

Soak the artichokes in a bowl of cold water with the lemon cut in half and squeezed for ½ hour. Soak the fresh peas in a bowl of cold water with the flour for ½ hour (this will tenderize the peas).

Cut the *pancetta* or prosciutto into tiny pieces. Coarsely chop the garlic.

Remove the artichokes from the bowl but preserve the water. Clean the artichokes (see page 122).

Heat the oil in a skillet over medium heat and, when it is warm, add the garlic and *pancetta* or prosciutto. Sauté for 5 minutes, stirring every so often. Drain the peas, rinse them under cold running water to remove all of the flour and add them to the skillet. Drain the artichoke pieces and spread them out over the peas, without mixing. Cover and cook for 2 minutes.

Add ½ cup of the broth to the skillet, season with salt and pepper, still without mixing, cover again and cook for 5 minutes more. Mix very well, add another ½ cup of broth and continue to cook, adding broth as more liquid is needed, always replacing the lid. When all the broth is incorporated (after about 10 minutes), the peas and artichokes should be cooked but still firm. Sprinkle on the parsley and mix very well. Transfer to a serving dish and serve hot.

SERVES 6 TO 8

A display of dried beans: back row left,
borlotti, *right,* piattellini; *middle left,*
toscanelli, *center,* fagioli con l'occhio *(black-
eyed peas), right,* lentils; *front row left,* ceci
(chick peas) and right, cannellini.

FAGIOLI STUFATI
Tuscan Beans Baked with Tuna and Lemon

2 cups dried *cannellini* beans
4½ cups cold water
10 large sage leaves, fresh or preserved in salt (see page 122)
4 tablespoons olive oil
4 large cloves garlic, peeled but left whole
4 ounces *pancetta* or prosciutto, in one piece
Freshly ground black pepper

PLUS
1 7-ounce can tuna, preserved in olive oil, drained
1 large lemon
Salt to taste

TO SERVE
Freshly ground black pepper
10 sprigs Italian parsley, leaves only

Soak the beans overnight in a large bowl of cold water.

The next morning, preheat the oven to 400 degrees.

Drain the beans, rinse them very well and place them in a heavy ovenproof casserole or in a traditional terra-cotta *fagioliera*. Pour in the water, then add the sage along with the olive oil, garlic, *pancetta* or prosciutto and freshly ground black pepper to taste. Cover the casserole and bake for about 2 hours, stirring the beans twice. (The cooking time for beans can vary a lot, depending on their dryness and the method that was used to dry them.)

When the beans are almost cooked, place the tuna in a small crockery or glass bowl, squeeze the juice of the lemon over it and mix very well.

Remove the cooked beans from the oven, add the tuna mixture and salt and pepper to taste and bake, uncovered, for 10 minutes.

Remove from the oven and serve with freshly ground black pepper and parsley sprinkled over each serving.

SERVES 8 TO 10

FOCACCIA DI PATATE
Stuffed Potato Focaccia

Coarse-grained salt
1½ pounds boiling potatoes (not new potatoes)
4 tablespoons (2 ounces) sweet butter
1 cup warm milk
Salt and freshly ground black pepper
3 sweet bell peppers (of different colors, if possible)
1 medium-sized red onion, cleaned
1 clove garlic, peeled
4 tablespoons olive oil
A large pinch of hot red pepper flakes

2 extra-large eggs
1 extra-large egg yolk
5 tablespoons freshly grated *parmigiano-reggiano*

PLUS

5 tablespoons very fine unseasoned bread crumbs, preferably homemade, lightly toasted
4 tablespoons capers in wine vinegar, drained

Bring a large pot of cold water to a boil over medium heat, and add coarse-grained salt to taste.

Add the potatoes to the boiling water and cook for ½ hour, or until soft. Drain and peel the potatoes while still hot, then pass them through a potato ricer into a crockery or glass bowl.

Melt the butter in a saucepan over low heat, then add the riced potatoes and stir constantly with a wooden spoon until the butter is completely incorporated. Stir the warm milk into the potatoes until completely absorbed, about 2 minutes. Season lightly with salt and pepper, then transfer to a crockery or glass bowl to cool for 1 hour.

Wash the peppers well and remove the stems, ribs and seeds. Then cut them into ½-inch rings and place them in a bowl of cold water. Cut the onion into ½-inch rings, place them in the bowl with the peppers and soak for 1 hour.

Meanwhile, cut the garlic into small pieces on a board.

When ready, drain the peppers and onions, and put them in a saucepan with the garlic and oil. Sprinkle with salt and pepper, add the red pepper flakes, cover the pan and place it over medium heat. Cook for 40 minutes. Then stir the ingredients together and, using a slotted spoon, transfer the pepper-onion mixture to a crockery or glass bowl to cool for ½ hour. Discard the remaining cooking liquid.

Preheat the oven to 375 degrees. Lightly butter a 10-inch glass pie plate and line it with the bread crumbs.

Add the eggs, egg yolk and *parmigiano-reggiano* to the cooled potatoes, mix thoroughly and taste for salt and pepper. Cover the bottom and sides of the pie plate with two thirds of the potato mixture. Arrange the pepper-onion mixture inside this potato shell and scatter the capers on top of the mixture. Top with a layer of the remaining potatoes. Bake for 40 minutes. Remove from the oven and let stand for 2 to 3 minutes.

Place a serving plate upside down over the *focaccia* and hold it in place while reversing the pie plate. Lift off the pie plate, leaving the *focaccia* upside down on the serving dish. Cover with another serving dish, reverse and lift off the top so the *focaccia* emerges right side up. To serve, slice the *focaccia* like a pie.

SERVES 8

Young, tender string beans, long zucchini, delicate zucchini blossoms and fresh porcini *mushrooms on proud display in the Florence market.*

PATATE CON FINOCCHIO
Potatoes with Fennel

1 fennel bulb
5 tablespoons olive oil
2 medium-sized cloves garlic, peeled but left whole
1 cup meat or chicken broth, preferably homemade
  Salt and freshly ground black pepper

2 pounds boiling potatoes (not new potatoes)
1 cup lukewarm water

TO SERVE
15 sprigs Italian parsley, leaves only
   Freshly ground black pepper

Clean the fennel bulb, removing the tough outer leaves. Cut the bulb into 1-inch pieces. Soak in a bowl of cold water for ½ hour; then drain and carefully wash under cold running water.

Heat the oil in a medium-sized skillet over low heat and, when the oil is warm, add the garlic and fennel. Sauté for 2 minutes, stirring every so often with a wooden spoon. Then add the broth, cover the skillet and cook for at least 25 minutes, until the fennel is very soft and almost all of the broth is incorporated. Season with salt and pepper, stir and cook for 1 minute more.

Meanwhile, peel the potatoes and cut them into 2-inch cubes.

Add the potatoes to the skillet, without mixing, sprinkle with salt and pepper, cover and cook for 5 minutes. Add the lukewarm water, mix very gently, cover again and cook for 15 minutes more, mixing twice. The potatoes should be cooked but still retain their shape. Transfer the contents of the skillet to a serving platter and sprinkle with parsley and black pepper. Serve hot or at room temperature.

SERVES 4 TO 6

OPPOSITE:
On the steps of the Rialto wholesale market, a Venetian shopkeeper loads purchases onto his boat.

PEPERONATA ALL'ARRABBIATA
Spicy Peperonata

8 large sweet bell peppers of different colors
2 medium-sized red onions, cleaned
2 medium-sized cloves garlic, peeled
½ cup olive oil
  Salt and freshly ground black pepper
½ teaspoon hot red pepper flakes

5 heaping tablespoons capers in wine vinegar, drained

TO SERVE
20 sprigs Italian parsley, leaves only, coarsely chopped

Clean the peppers, discarding the stems and seeds.

Cut into strips less than ½ inch wide. Soak the strips in a bowl of cold water for ½ hour.

Coarsely chop the onions and finely chop the garlic on a board.

Heat the oil in a medium-sized casserole over medium heat and, when the oil is warm, add the chopped ingredients. Lower the heat and sauté for 20 minutes, stirring occasionally with a wooden spoon.

Drain the peppers and add them to the casserole.

Season with salt and pepper and the red pepper flakes, then raise the heat and sauté for 5 minutes, stirring very well. Lower the heat, cover the casserole and cook for 15 minutes more, mixing every so often. The peppers should be cooked through but still fairly firm. Rinse the capers under cold running water, add them to the casserole, mix very well and cook for 2 minutes more.

Transfer the contents of the casserole to a large warmed serving platter, and sprinkle the parsley all over. Serve hot or at room temperature.

SERVES 6 TO 8

DESSERTS

LIQUORE AL MANDARINO
Orange Liqueur

3 mandarin oranges or tangerines
1 quart pure grain alcohol or unflavored vodka

3 cups water
3 cups granulated sugar (see Note)

Wrap the oranges in a piece of cheesecloth and tie the package together with string, leaving about 5 inches of string on each side of the knot.

Pour the alcohol into a 3-quart mason jar. Holding the cheesecloth package by the string, hang it in the jar so that it is dangling over but is not touching the alcohol. Wrap the string around the mouth of the jar and tie it tightly in order to keep the cheesecloth package in place. Close the jar tightly and put the jar in a dark place for 1 month.

After a month, prepare a sugar syrup: Put the water in a small saucepan and heat it over medium heat until it comes to a boil. Then add the sugar and simmer for about 5 minutes. Remove the pan from the heat and let the syrup cool completely, about 2 hours.

Remove the oranges from the jar and pour the liqueur into a bottle. Add the cooled syrup to the bottle and let stand for 3 hours. Use a coffee filter to filter the liqueur into another bottle. Cork the bottle and let the liqueur stand for 3 days before using it.

To prepare punch, place about ¼ cup of the liqueur in a cup and heat it with the steam of an espresso coffee machine, using the spout that produces the foam for cappuccino. Serve immediately with a piece of orange peel.

MAKES ABOUT 2 QUARTS

Note: You will need the steam spout of a cappucino
machine to prepare the punch for this recipe.

Homemade Liquore al mandarino *(Orange Liqueur). The cheesecloth suspends the oranges just above the alcohol.*

PERE RIPIENE AL CIOCCOLATO
Pears Stuffed with Cream and Chocolate

FOR THE PEARS

6 large ripe but not overripe Bosc pears
   Juice of 1 lemon
3 cups dry white wine
1 strip lemon peel (about 2 inches long)
   Juice of 3 oranges
2 whole cloves
1 cup granulated sugar

FOR THE STUFFING

4 to 5 shelled unsalted fresh pistachio nuts
   Coarse-grained salt
4 tablespoons (2 ounces) sweet butter

1 heaping tablespoon unsweetened cocoa
   powder
4 tablespoons granulated sugar
3 tablespoons cold water
½ cup heavy cream
1 tablespoon confectioners' sugar

FOR THE *SALSA AL CIOCCOLATO*

2 ounces baker's chocolate, cut into small pieces
½ cup granulated sugar
4 tablespoons cold water
4 tablespoons brandy
½ cup heavy cream

Peel the pears, leaving the stems on. Slice off the bottom of each pear so they can stand on the flat end. With a paring knife, cut out the core and seeds from the bottom end of each pear, leaving the pears whole. Be careful not to disturb the stem end.

Fill the cavity of each pear with aluminum foil. Stand the pears in a small saucepan and pour in the lemon juice, white wine and enough water to cover the fruit up to the stems. Add the lemon peel, orange juice, cloves and sugar to the pan. Put the pan over medium heat and bring it to a simmer. Then lower the heat and simmer, covered, until the pears are cooked but still retain their shape, about 20 minutes, depending on the ripeness of the pears.

Transfer the pears to a serving dish so that they are standing up. Cover the dish with aluminum foil and let stand until the pears are cool.

Remove the lemon peel and cloves from the poaching liquid and reduce it over low heat until a very thick syrup is formed, about 1½ hours. Then transfer the syrup to a crockery or glass bowl to cool completely.

Prepare the stuffing: Blanch the pistachio nuts in salted boiling water for a few seconds. Then drain the nuts and coarsely chop them.

Put the butter, cocoa powder, granulated sugar and water in a small saucepan. Holding the pan at the edge of the burner, stir with a wooden spoon until all of the ingredients are amalgamated. Simmer for about 10 minutes, until a cocoa syrup has formed. Remove from the heat and let stand until cool.

Using a chilled metal bowl and a wire whisk, whip the heavy cream with the confectioners' sugar until stiff. Refrigerate the whipped cream until needed.

Prepare the sauce: Melt the chocolate with the sugar and water in a small saucepan over low heat. Stir very well until the chocolate is completely melted and the sugar is dissolved, 5 to 6 minutes. Then add the brandy and heavy cream and stir very well with a wooden spoon. Transfer the chocolate sauce to a bottle and refrigerate for about 1 hour.

When the pears and both syrups are cool, remove the whipped cream from the refrigerator. Stir in the cooled cocoa syrup and the chopped pistachio nuts until well combined.

Carefully remove the aluminum foil from the cavity of each pear and fill each cavity with the whipped cream mixture. Stand the pears on a serving platter lined with a piece of wax paper and refrigerate for at least ½ hour.

When the pears are chilled, use a spatula to transfer them to individual plates. Brush them with the cooled wine syrup, pour the chocolate sauce around them and serve.

SERVES 6

109

PANNA COTTA
"Cooked Cream" Molds

3½ cups cold heavy cream
½ vanilla bean (not split)
1½ teaspoons unflavored gelatin
½ cup granulated sugar
2 tablespoons light rum

PLUS
1½ cups heavy cream

1 tablespoon confectioners' sugar
Rum to moisten 8 *baba* molds or custard
cups

OPTIONAL
Assorted berries, mixed with granulated
sugar for sweetness if desired

Rinse out a medium-sized saucepan with cold water, then add 2 cups of the heavy cream, along with the vanilla bean; this keeps the cream from sticking to the pan as it heats up. Set the pan over medium heat and simmer, stirring every so often with a wooden spoon, until the cream is reduced by ½ cup.

When the cream is almost ready, sprinkle the gelatin over the remaining 1½ cups of cold heavy cream and let rest for about 5 minutes. Then pour the heavy cream with the dissolved gelatin into a blender or food processor along with the sugar and light rum.

Immediately strain the simmering cream into the cold cream, discarding the vanilla bean, and blend everything together for about 2 minutes. Then transfer the cream mixture to a crockery or glass bowl and let rest until cool, about 15 minutes.

Meanwhile, moisten the 8 *baba* molds or custard cups with the rum.

After the cream mixture has cooled, use a chilled metal bowl and a wire whisk to whip the 1½ cups cream with the confectioners' sugar. Fold the whipped cream into the cooled cream, then pour the mixture into the *baba* molds, filling each one three-quarters full. Cover the molds with plastic wrap and refrigerate for at least 3 hours, or until the cream sets.

Unmold each cream onto an individual plate and serve, surrounded by the berries if using.

SERVES 8

TIRAMISÙ
"Lift Me Up"

FOR THE *CREMA*

6 extra-large egg yolks, at room temperature
6 heaping tablespoons granulated sugar
¾ cup milk

PLUS

1 pound *mascarpone* cheese or ½ pound ricotta plus 1 cup heavy cream, blended very well in a food processor until a light cream forms
8 ounces bittersweet chocolate
24 very crisp Italian ladyfingers
2 cups heavy cream
1 tablespoon granulated sugar
1 teaspoon confectioners' sugar
2 cups strong espresso coffee, cooled

Bring water to a boil in the bottom of a double boiler.

Combine the egg yolks and sugar in a crockery or glass bowl and stir with a wooden spoon until the sugar is completely dissolved and the egg yolks turn a lighter color. Add the milk and mix thoroughly. Transfer the egg mixture to the top part of the double boiler and insert it over the boiling water. Stir constantly with a wooden spoon, always in the same direction, until the cream is thick enough to coat the spoon, just before the mixture is about to start to boil. Absolutely do not allow the mixture to boil. Immediately remove the top part of the double boiler from the heat. Continue to stir for 1 minute longer, then transfer the crema to a crockery or glass bowl to cool, about 1 hour.

Place the *mascarpone* or ricotta cream mixture in the bowl of a food processor, add the cooled *crema* and blend very well until a very smooth and light cream forms. Refrigerate until needed.

Chop the chocolate coarsely. Place the ladyfingers in one layer in a jelly-roll pan.

Whip the heavy cream, granulated sugar and confectioners' sugar in a chilled metal bowl with a wire whisk. Add the cooled *crema-mascarpone* and whisk very well.

Soak the ladyfingers with the cold coffee and gently transfer 12 of them to a 14-inch "trifle" bowl. Spread half of the cream on top of the ladyfingers, then sprinkle on half of the chocolate. Make one more layer with the remaining ingredients, then cover with plastic wrap and refrigerate for at least 1 hour before serving.

SERVES 12

TORTA AL MARSALA CON FRAGOLE
Marsala Tart with Strawberries

FOR THE CRUST
4   ounces plus 2 tablespoons unbleached all-purpose flour
4   tablespoons (2 ounces) sweet butter
4   tablespoons dry Marsala wine
    Pinch of salt

FOR THE *ZABAIONE* FILLING
5   extra-large egg yolks, at room temperature

5   tablespoons granulated sugar
¼   cup light rum
¼   cup dry Marsala wine

PLUS
1   pint heavy cream
2   heaping tablespoons granulated sugar
1   teaspoon confectioners' sugar
2   pints strawberries, hulled

Prepare the crust: Sift the flour onto a pastry board and arrange it in a mound. Cut the butter into pieces and lay them over the mound. Let the butter stand for ½ hour to soften.

Start mixing the butter into the flour with your fingers. Then rub the flour and butter between your palms until well amalgamated. Make a well in the butter-flour mixture and put the Marsala and salt in the well. Start mixing with a fork, pushing the butter-flour mixture in from the rim of the well, until all the Marsala is incorporated. Begin to form a ball with your hands, incorporating the dough stuck to the fork. Knead gently until a very smooth and elastic ball of dough is formed, 2 minutes. Dampen a cotton dish towel and wrap the ball of dough in it. Let rest in a cool place for 1 hour.

Butter a 9½-inch tart pan with a removable bottom.

Dust a pastry board with a little flour. Unwrap the dough and knead it for a few seconds. Then, using a rolling pin, roll out the dough into a round about 16 inches in diameter. Roll up the dough onto the rolling pin and unroll it over the buttered pan. Gently press the dough down into the bottom and up the sides of the pan. Cut off the overhanging pastry by moving the rolling pin over the pan. Use a fork to make several punctures in the pastry to keep it from puffing up. Fit a sheet of aluminum foil loosely over the pastry and put weights or dried beans on the foil to keep the shell from rising while it bakes. Refrigerate the prepared pastry for 15 minutes.

Preheat the oven to 375 degrees.

Bake the pastry for ½ hour. Remove it from the oven, lift out the foil containing the weights and return the shell to the oven for 10 minutes longer. Remove from the oven and let the crust cool in the pan for 1 hour.

Prepare the *zabaione*: Put water in the bottom of a double boiler and bring to a boil.

Place the egg yolks in a crockery or glass bowl and add the sugar. Stir with a wooden spoon, always in the same direction, until the sugar is completely dissolved and the egg yolks turn a lighter color.

Slowly add the rum and Marsala, mixing steadily. Then transfer the contents of the bowl to the top part of the double boiler and insert it over the boiling water in the bottom part of the double boiler. Stir the egg mixture constantly with a wooden spoon, always in the same direction. The moment before the mixture is about to start boiling, when it is thick enough to coat the wooden spoon, remove it from the heat and stir for 1 minute more. Transfer the *zabaione* to a crockery or glass bowl and let stand until cool, then cover and refrigerate until cold, about ½ hour.

Preheat the oven to 375 degrees.

Pour the cold *zabaione* into the cooled pastry shell and spread it out evenly. Place the shell in the oven for 5 minutes. Remove the shell from the oven and transfer it to a rack. Let stand until completely cool, about ½ hour.

Using a chilled metal bowl and a wire whisk, whip the cream until stiff, adding the granulated sugar and the confectioners' sugar.

Remove the shell from the tart pan and transfer it to a serving dish. Arrange the strawberries all around the edge of the tart. Use a pastry bag to mound the whipped cream in the center of the tart, leaving a space between the cream and the ring of strawberries. Slice and serve.

SERVES 6 TO 8

113

CILIEGE AL VINO ROSSO
Cherries Baked in Red Wine

2 pounds ripe but not overripe cherries, stems removed

3 cups full-bodied red wine

2 tablespoons granulated sugar

1 tablespoon confectioners' sugar

2 tablespoons brandy or rum

TO SERVE

   Sprigs of fresh mint

Preheat the oven to 375 degrees.

Wash the cherries very well and place them in a glass baking dish. Pour the wine over the cherries and sprinkle with the sugars. The wine should cover the cherries completely. Bake for 45 minutes, until the cherries are cooked through but still firm. Add the brandy and bake for 5 minutes more.

Transfer the fruit to a serving platter, using a slot-ted spoon, and pour the wine into a medium-sized casserole. Place the casserole over medium heat and simmer until the wine is reduced by half, about 35 minutes. Pour the reduced wine over the cherries and let rest until cool, about 1 hour.

Serve with sprigs of fresh mint. (This dish is even better if prepared one or two days in advance and allowed to rest, covered, in the refrigerator.)

SERVES 8 TO 10

TORTA DI CILIEGE
Cherry Torte

FOR THE CUSTARD CREAM

6 extra-large egg yolks, at room temperature
6 tablespoons granulated sugar
1½ cups cold heavy cream
1 cup lukewarm milk

FOR THE TORTE

1 pound pitted large sweet cherries or 2 cans (totaling 17 ounces) pitted dark sweet cherries in extra-heavy syrup
12 ounces whole-milk ricotta
4 ounces champagne puffs, tea biscuits or any other sweet, very crisp biscuits
Grated peel of 1 large orange (with thick skin)

PLUS

1 tablespoon sweet butter
2 tablespoons confectioners' sugar

Prepare the custard: Bring water to a boil in the bottom of a double boiler.

Put the egg yolks and sugar in a crockery or glass bowl and stir with a wooden spoon, always in the same direction, until the sugar is completely dissolved and the egg yolks turn a lighter color. Slowly add the cold heavy cream, then the lukewarm milk, mixing steadily. Transfer the contents of the bowl to the top part of a double boiler and insert the top over the boiling water. Stir constantly with a wooden spoon, always in the same direction, until the custard cream is thick enough to coat the spoon, just before the mixture is about to start to boil. Absolutely do not allow the mixture to boil. Immediately remove the top of the double boiler from the heat. Continue to stir the cream for 1 minute longer, then transfer it to a crockery bowl to cool completely, about 1 hour.

Meanwhile, prepare the torte: Preheat the oven to 375 degrees.

If using canned cherries, drain them and let stand in a colander until needed in order to drain all remaining syrup.

Pass the ricotta through a very fine strainer into a large crockery bowl.

Finely grind the tea biscuits. Add ¾ cup of the ground biscuits and the grated orange peel to the bowl containing the ricotta. Mix all the ingredients very well together, using a wooden spoon. With the tablespoon of butter, heavily butter a 10-inch springform pan and line it with the remaining ground biscuits.

When the custard cream is cool, add it to the large bowl with the other ingredients. Mix very well with a wooden spoon until all of the ingredients are well combined. Then add the cherries and gently mix them in. Pour the contents of the bowl into the prepared springform pan and bake for 1 hour. Remove the pan from the oven, place it on a rack and let cool for 1 hour.

Transfer the cooled torte to a large round serving dish. Using a strainer, sprinkle the top of the torte with the confectioners' sugar. Slice and serve.

SERVES 6 TO 8

PESCHE ALLA MENTA
Marinated Whole Peaches with Mint

Coarse-grained salt
8 large perfect ripe but not overripe peaches (with no blemishes)
4 to 5 cups dry white wine
½ cup brandy

3 tablespoons granulated sugar
4 or more large fresh mint sprigs

TO SERVE
Fresh mint leaves

Bring a large pot of cold water to a boil over medium heat, and add a pinch of coarse salt. Add the peaches to the boiling water and blanch for 1 to 3 minutes, depending on the type of peaches you are using and the season. Carefully transfer the peaches from the boiling water to a bowl of cold water.

Use a paring knife to carefully remove the skin from the peaches. When the first peach is ready, place it in a crockery or glass bowl and immediately pour 4 cups of wine and the brandy over it. When all the peaches are in the bowl, add more wine if they are not completely covered. Add the sugar and at least 4 sprigs of mint, cover the bowl and refrigerate for at least 5 to 6 hours before serving.

When ready to serve, discard the mint from the marinade. Serve each peach with some of the marinade and a fresh mint leaf.

SERVES 8

DOLCE DI CAFFÈ
Coffee-Nut Cake

FOR THE CAKE
½ cup strong coffee, preferably Italian espresso
4 tablespoons unsweetened cocoa powder
4 extra-large eggs, separated
7 tablespoons granulated sugar
3 ounces blanched almonds
4 ounces walnuts

FOR THE COFFEE *ZABAIONE*
3 extra-large egg yolks, at room temperature
4 tablespoons granulated sugar
½ cup cold strong coffee, preferably Italian espresso

PLUS
1¼ cups heavy cream
3 tablespoons granulated sugar
1 tablespoon confectioner' sugar

Prepare the cake: Preheat the oven to 375 degrees.

Lightly butter and flour an 8-inch soufflé dish.

Heat the coffee over medium heat until lukewarm. Place the cocoa powder in a small bowl, then pour in the coffee and stir very well with a wooden spoon until the cocoa is completely dissolved. Let stand until cool, about ½ hour.

Place the egg yolks in a crockery or glass bowl. Add 4 tablespoons of the sugar and stir very well with a wooden spoon until the sugar is completely dissolved and the egg yolks turn a lighter color. Add the cooled coffee-cocoa mixture and stir very well, then transfer the contents of the bowl to a large bowl and let stand until needed.

Using a knife, *mezzaluna* or food processor, finely grind together the almonds, walnuts and the remaining 3 tablespoons sugar. Add to the bowl with the egg mixture.

Using a copper bowl and wire whisk, beat the egg whites until stiff. Using a wooden spoon, gently fold in the egg-nut mixture, in a rotating motion. Pour this batter into the prepared dish and bake for 45 minutes.

Meanwhile, prepare the coffee *zabaione*: Put water in the bottom of a double boiler and bring to a boil.

Place the egg yolks in a crockery or glass bowl and add the sugar. Stir with a wooden spoon, always in the same direction, until the sugar is completely dissolved and the egg yolks turn a lighter color. Slowly add the coffee, mixing steadily. Transfer the contents of the bowl to the top part of the double boiler, and insert it over the boiling water in the bottom part of the double boiler. Stir the egg mixture constantly with a wooden spoon, always in the same direction. The moment before the mixture is about to start boiling, when it is thick enough to coat the wooden spoon, remove it from the heat and stir for 1 minute more. Transfer the *zabaione* to a crockery or glass bowl and let stand until cool. Then cover and refrigerate until cold, about ½ hour.

When the *zabaione* has cooled, using a chilled metal bowl and wire whisk, whip the cream with the granulated sugar and confectioners' sugar. Fold the cooled *zabaione* into the whipped cream. Cover the bowl and refrigerate until needed.

Remove the soufflé dish from the oven, unmold the cake onto a rack and let cool for about 20 minutes (or longer if you wish to eat the cake cold).

Transfer the cooled cake onto a serving dish. Slice it and serve, placing some of the coffee-flavored *crema zabaione* on one side of each piece.

LIMONI IN FORMA
Lemon Timbales

FOR THE TIMBALES

2 cups heavy cream

1 cup milk

Grated peel of 3 large lemons (with thick skin)

4 ounces tea biscuits, champagne puffs or any other sweet, very crisp biscuits

4 extra-large eggs, at room temperature

2 extra-large egg yolks, at room temperature

3 ounces confectioners' sugar

8 tablespoons (4 ounces) sweet butter, at room temperature

2 tablespoons light rum

1 tablespoon potato starch (not potato flour)

TO BAKE THE TIMBALES

Sweet butter to butter the molds

6 teaspoons granulated sugar to line the molds, plus extra to sprinkle over the timbales

FOR THE CUSTARD CREAM

4 extra-large egg yolks, at room temperature

6 tablespoons granulated sugar

1 cup heavy cream

1 cup lukewarm milk

1 teaspoon domestic lemon extract or, preferably, 2 drops imported (without water or alcohol)

TO SERVE

Lemon zests (see page 122)

Rinse out a medium-sized casserole with cold water, then pour in the heavy cream and milk; this keeps the milk and heavy cream from sticking to the bottom of the casserole as it heats up. Add the grated lemon peel to the casserole. Set the casserole over medium heat and simmer the milk mixture for ½ hour, stirring every so often with a wooden spoon to break the skin that forms. Strain the contents of the casserole through a very fine strainer into a crockery or glass bowl, and let the mixture cool for at least ½ hour.

Preheat the oven to 375 degrees. Prepare a pan for a water bath: Place a cotton dish towel or paper towels on the bottom of a baking dish. Lightly but-ter 12 custard cups and line them with sugar.

Finely grind the biscuits in a food processor or blender.

Place the eggs and egg yolks in a crockery or glass bowl and mix together. Add the confectioners' sugar and mix very well with a wooden spoon, stirring until the sugar is completely dissolved and the eggs are much lighter in color. Add the butter, rum and potato starch and mix again until the butter is absorbed and the mixture is very light and full of air. Gradually incorporate the cooled milk, alternating with the ground biscuits.

Fill the prepared custard cups two-thirds full with the batter and place the cups in the prepared

*Lemon trees abound in southern Italy where the fruit is
a favorite cooking ingredient.*

baking dish. Pour enough lukewarm water into the baking dish to reach almost the level of the batter in the cups. Bake for 25 minutes. Sprinkle ½ teaspoon sugar over each timbale and bake for 20 minutes more.

Meanwhile, prepare the custard cream: Bring water to a boil in the bottom of a double boiler.

Put the egg yolks in a crockery or glass bowl. Add the sugar and stir, always in the same direction, with a wooden spoon, until the sugar is completely dissolved and the egg yolks turn a light yellow color. Slowly add the cream, milk and lemon extract, stirring constantly. Transfer the cream mixture to the top part of the double boiler and insert over the boil-ing water in the bottom part of the double boiler. Cook, stirring constantly, always in the same direction, until thick enough to coat the spoon. Do not allow to boil. Immediately remove the top part of the double boiler from the heat and continue to stir for 2 to 3 minutes. Transfer the cream to a crockery or glass bowl and let cool for a few minutes, then transfer it to an empty wine bottle, cork it and refrigerate until needed. (You can serve the cream lukewarm or cold.)

When ready, remove the timbales from the oven, unmold onto individual dishes and pour some of the custard cream over them. Serve hot, with lemon zests arranged over the timbales.

SERVES 12

119

FRUTTA IN PADELLA CON SALSA ALLA VANIGLIA
Sautéed Fruit with Vanilla Sauce

FOR THE SAUCE
2 cups cold milk
1 piece vanilla bean (about 2 inches)
6 extra-large egg yolks, at room temperature
6 ounces granulated sugar
1 cup heavy cream

FOR THE FRUIT
2 cups dry white wine

2 tablespoons freshly squeezed lemon juice
4 ripe but not overripe Bosc pears or 1 pound dried apricots or peaches (see Note)
4 tablespoons (2 ounces) sweet butter
5 tablespoons granulated sugar
1 teaspoon domestic orange extract or, preferably, 1 drop imported (without water or alcohol)
½ cup brandy

Prepare the sauce: Rinse out a heavy casserole with cold water, then pour in the milk; this keeps the milk from sticking to the bottom of the casserole as it heats up. Add the piece of vanilla bean. Bring to a boil over medium heat and cook for about 5 minutes, stirring every so often.

Meanwhile, bring water to a boil in the botom of a double boiler.

Put the egg yolks in a crockery or glass bowl and add the sugar. Stir with a wooden spoon, always in the same direction, until the sugar is completely dissolved and the egg yolks turn a lighter color. Slowly add the heavy cream, mixing steadily.

When the milk is ready, pass it through a strainer into a bowl, and discard the vanilla bean. Immediately add the strained hot milk to the bowl containing the egg yolks, and mix very well with a wooden spoon. Then transfer the contents of the bowl to the top of the double boiler and place it over the boiling water in the bottom. Stir constantly with a wooden spoon, always in the same direction, until the mixture is thick enough to coat the spoon, just before the mixture is about to start to boil. Absolutely do not allow the mixture to boil! When the mixture coats the spoon, immediately remove the top part of the double boiler from the heat. Continue to stir for 2 or 3 minutes longer, then transfer the cream to a crockery bowl and let cool for about 15 minutes, stirring every so often with the wooden spoon. Pour the cream into a wine bottle, cork it and place on the bottom shelf of the refrigerator for about 1 hour, or until needed. (The sauce can be prepared up to 2 days in advance.)

Prepare the fruit: Pour the wine and 1 tablespoon of the lemon juice into a crockery or glass bowl.

If using pears, peel them with a peeler. If using dried fruit, drain it. Cut the fruit lengthwise into quarters or eighths, depending on the size. Remove the cores, if any, put the fruit in the crockery bowl with the wine-lemon juice mixture and let marinate for about ½ hour.

Chill six serving dishes.

Place the butter in a large skillet over medium heat. When the butter is melted, transfer the fruit, with a strainer-skimmer, to the skillet. Save the soaking wine. Gently sauté the fruit for about 5 minutes, mixing with a large spoon to be sure the butter coats the fruit thoroughly. If the fruit is still not soft after 5 minutes, add ¼ cup of the soaking wine and let it reduce while the fruit softens. When the fruit is cooked through but still retains its shape, sprinkle with the sugar, then the remaining tablespoon of lemon juice and the orange extract. Cook, turning the fruit, until it is completely coated with a light layer of golden-colored caramelized sugar, about 4 minutes. Add the brandy and let it evaporate, mixing continuously with a wooden spoon, about 2 minutes. Remove from the heat, and serve immediately. Place some of the hot fruit in the center of each chilled dish and surround with a thin ring of the chilled cream.

SERVES 6

Note: If using dried fruit, soak it for several hours before beginning the sauce.

APPENDIX

Cleaning Artichokes

Cut off the ends of the stems. Trim off all of the darker outer skin of the stems. Remove as many rows of the outer leaves as necessary until you arrive at those leaves in which you can see the separation between the green at the top and the light yellow at the bottom. Remove the top green part by pressing your thumb on the bottom yellow part of each leaf and, with your other hand, tearing off the top green part. When you reach the rows in which only the very top part of the leaves are green, cut off these tips completely with a knife.

To remove the hair and the choke, first cut all around the choke with a knife, then scoop out the choke and the attached hair, using a long-handled teaspoon. As each artichoke is cleaned, return it to the bowl with the acidulated water until needed.

Grating Oranges and Lemons

Place a piece of parchment paper or thick waxed paper over the holes of a hand grater. Hold the paper in place with one hand while moving the orange or lemon back and forth on the paper with the other. Work on different sections of the paper so that the paper does not wear out. Use a rubber spatula to remove the grated orange or lemon peel from the paper. Do not use what is inside the grater or any of the bitter white part of the peel.

Making Orange or Lemon Zests

Orange or lemon zests, thin strips of the colored part of the fruit, can be made most easily with a citrus zester or a vegetable peeler. Simply pull the zester from the top of the fruit to the base so that you end up with long thin strips of zest. It is important not to catch any of the white pith, as it has a bitter flavor. Strips of zest can be cut from the fruit with a knife, although it is more difficult to make thin strips and to avoid the white pith.

Preserving Aromatic Herbs in Salt

Remove the leaves of the herbs from their stems, without washing them. In a mason jar, make a ½-inch-thick layer of coarse-grained salt. Add a layer of herb leaves, then salt, and continue in this manner until all the leaves are used up or the jar is full, finishing with a layer of salt. Close the jar securely and keep in a cool place. To use the herbs, wash away the salt and any dirt that may be clinging to the leaves. Some herbs, such as basil, will lose some of their color, but they will not lose any of their flavor.

Dried and Blanched Rosemary Leaves

If you do not have fresh rosemary leaves or rosemary preserved in salt, blanch dried leaves in boiling water for a few seconds. Use the same quantity of blanched leaves as you would fresh.

Making Pasta by Hand or with a Manual Pasta Machine

To prepare the pasta dough, place the flour in a mound on a pasta board. Use a fork to make a well in the center. Place the eggs and salt and any other ingredients specified in the recipe in the well, and mix them together with a fork. Then, still using the fork, begin to incorporate the flour from the inside of the well, always incorporating fresh flour from the lower part of the well and pushing it under the dough that is forming to keep it from sticking to the board. Remove any pieces of dough that stick to the fork and incorporate them. Then gather the dough together and set to one side of the board. Scrape the board with a pastry scraper, gathering together all the unincorporated flour, and sprinkle this flour over the board.

Start kneading the dough on the board, using the palm of one hand and folding the dough over with the other hand. (The dough will gradually absorb more of the flour; do not sprinkle flour over the dough.) Continue kneading until the dough is no longer wet and all but 4 to 5 tablespoons of the flour have been incorporated into the dough: If you intend to stretch the dough by hand, knead for about 5 minutes; if you intend to use a pasta machine, knead for only 2 to 3 minutes. The dough should now be smooth and elastic.

To stretch the dough by hand, using a rolling pin: First knead the dough for an additional 10 minutes, incorporating some but not all of the flour remaining on the board. Then place the center of the rolling pin over the ball of dough and gently roll the pin forward, then backward. This is the basic rolling motion, which should be repeated until the dough is thin and elastic.

To stretch the dough to an even thickness, fold the edge of dough closest to you up over the rolling pin and roll up the sheet of dough around the pin, moving your fingers from the center outward along the edge of the pasta sheet to even out the edges. Then, with a quick, jerky movement, roll the pin one or two turns away from you so that the edge of the pasta sheet slaps against the board (this stretches the edge of the sheet). Flip the pin over and unroll the sheet away from you so that the underside is now on top.

As you roll out the pasta, alternate the back-and-forth motion with a side-to-side stretching motion. Turn so that you are working at a right angle to your original position, and roll the pin backward, then forward across the dough from this angle until the sheet is stretched to a little less than $1/8$ inch thick. Roll up the sheet over the pin, flip the pin over and unroll the sheet so that the underside is on top. Continue rolling and stretching the pasta sheet until it is less than $1/16$ inch thick, or the thinness specified in the recipe.

To stretch the dough using a manual pasta machine (if the pasta dough is made from more than 2 eggs, divide the dough into roughly 1-cup pieces and stretch each piece separately), With the palm of your hand, flatten the ball of dough to a thickness of about $1/2$ inch. Set the rollers at the widest setting, and pass the dough through the rollers. Lightly flour the dough on one side, fold it in thirds and press down to seal the three layers. Starting with an open end of the dough, pass through the rollers again. Repeat this folding and rolling 8 to 10 times, until the dough is smooth and elastic.

Set the rollers to the next thinnest setting, and roll the dough through the machine. Flour the pasta on both sides and pass through the next thinnest setting. Repeat flouring and rolling the dough until it is less than $1/16$ inch thick, or the thinness specified in the recipe (usually the last or next-to-the-last setting on the machine).

SOLID MEASURES CONVERSION CHART

U.S. AND IMPERIAL MEASURES		METRIC MEASURES	
Ounces	Pounds	Grams	Kilos
1		28	
2		56	
3½		100	
4	¼	112	
5		140	
6		168	
8	½	225	
9		250	¼
12	¾	340	
16	1	450	
18		500	½
20	1¼	560	
24	1½	675	
27		750	¾
28	1¾	780	
32	2	900	
36	2¼	1000	1
40	2½	1100	
48	3	1350	
54		1500	1½
64	4	1800	
72	4½	2000	2
80	5	2250	2¼
90		2500	2½
100	6	2800	2¾

OVEN TEMPERATURE EQUIVALENTS

Fahrenheit	Gas mark	Celsius	Heat of oven
225	¼	105	VERY COOL
250	½	120	VERY COOL
275	1	135	COOL
300	2	150	COOL
325	3	160	MODERATE
350	4	175	MODERATE
375	5	190	FAIRLY HOT
400	6	200	FAIRLY HOT
425	7	222	HOT
450	8	230	VERY HOT
475	9	245	VERY HOT

NOTE: *Oven temperatures are given as degrees Fahrenheit throughout the text.*

LIQUID MEASURES CONVERSION CHART

Fluid ounces	U.S. measures	Imperial measures	Milliliters
	1 TSP	1 TSP	5
¼	2 TSP	1 DESSERT-SPOON	7
½	1 TBS	1 TBS	15
1	2 TBS	2 TBS	28
2	¼ CUP	4 TBS	56
4	½ CUP OR ¼ PINT		110
5		¼ PINT OR 1 GILL	140
6	¾ CUP		170
8	1 CUP OR ½ PINT		225
9			250, ¼ LITER
10	1¼ CUPS	½ PINT	280
12	1½ CUPS OR ¾ PINT		340
15		¾ PINT	420
16	2 CUPS OR 1 PINT		450
18	2¼ CUPS		500, ½ LITER
20	2½ CUPS	1 PINT	560
24	3 CUPS OR 1½ PINTS		675
25		1¼ PINTS	700
27	3½ CUPS		750
30	3¾ CUPS	1½ PINTS	840
32	4 CUPS OR 2 PINTS OR 1 QUART		900
35		1¾ PINTS	980
36	4½ CUPS		1000, 1 LITER
40	5 CUPS OR 2½ PINTS	2 PINTS OR 1 QUART	1120
48	6 CUPS OR 3 PINTS		1350
50		2½ PINTS	1400
60	7½ CUPS	3 PINTS	1680
64	8 CUPS OR 4 PINTS OR 2 QUARTS		1800
72	9 CUPS		2000, 2 LITERS
80	10 CUPS OR 5 PINTS	4 PINTS	2250
96	12 CUPS OR 3 QUARTS		2700
100		5 PINTS	2800

NOTE: *All conversions are approximate. They have been rounded off to the nearest convenient measure.*

INDEX

Agnello alle erbe, 94

Appetizers, 9 - 27
  Bean Paste Canapés, 14 - 15
  Bread Salad, 22 - 23
  Bruschetta con ruchetta, 16 - 17
  Bruschetta with Arugula, 16 - 17
  Crostini di fagioli, 14 - 15
  Egg-White Frittata, 21
  Frittata di bianchi, 21
  Insalata di cappone, 18 - 19
  Insalata di peperoni e capperi, 10 - 11
  Marinated Capon Breast, 18 - 19
  Mozzarella Grilled on Skewers
    Roman-Style, 20
  Panzanella del Valdarno, 22 - 23
  Pepper Salad with Capers, 10 - 11
  Sage Batter Cake, 26 - 27
  Salviata, 26 - 27
  Spiedini alla romano, 20
  Tomato Tart, 24 - 25
  Torta di funghi, 12 - 13
  Torta di pomodoro, 24 - 25
  Wild Mushroom Tart, 12 - 13
Artichokes with Peas Roman-Style, 97

Bean-Barley Soup, 57
Bean Paste Canapés, 14 - 15
Bistecche di melanzane, 96
Breads, 16 - 17, 65 - 73
  Bread from Prato, 66 - 67
  Bruschetta con ruchetta, 16 - 17
  Bruschetta with Arugula, 16 - 17
  Focaccia al basilico, 70 - 71
  Focaccia with Basil, 70 - 71
  Grissini al ramerino, 72 - 73
  Pane di Prato, 66 - 67
  Rosemary Grissini, 72 - 73
  Schiacciata con uva, 68 - 69
  Schiacciata with Fresh Grapes, 68 - 69
Bread from Prato, 66 - 67
Bread Salad, 22 - 23
Bruschetta con ruchetta, 16 - 17
Bruschetta with Arugula, 16 - 17

Cacciucco con battuto alla livornese, 58 - 59
Canestrelli di Chioggia, 80
Carciofi e piselli alla romana, 97
Carpaccio, 81
Cherries Baked in Red Wine, 114
Cherry Torte, 115
Chicken Baked with Peppers, 87
Chicken and Veal Galantine-Sausage
    with Green Peppercorns, 84 - 85
Chicken Roasted with Lemon Halves, 86
Ciliege al vino rosso, 114
Coffee-Nut Cake, 117
"Cooked Cream" Molds, 110
Cornmeal-Buckwheat Polenta with Pork
    Stew, 92 - 93
Crostini di fagioli, 14 - 15

Desserts, 105 - 121
  Cherries Baked in Red Wine, 114
  Cherry Torte, 115
  Ciliege al vino rosso, 114
  Coffee-Nut Cake, 117
  "Cooked Cream" Molds, 110
  Dolce di caffè, 117
  *Frutta in padella con salsa alla
    vaniglia*, 120 - 121
  Lemon Timbales, 118 - 119
  "Lift Me Up," 111
  Limoni in forma, 118 - 119
  Liquore al mandarino, 106 - 107
  Marinated Whole Peaches with Mint, 116
  Marsala Tart with Strawberries, 112 - 113
  Orange Liqueur, 106 - 107
  Panna cotta, 110
  Pears Stuffed with Cream and
    Chocolate, 108 - 109
  Pere ripiene al cioccolato, 108 - 109
  Pesche alla menta, 116
  Sautéed Fruit with Vanilla Sauce,
    120 - 121
  Tiramisù, 111
  Torta al marsala con fragole, 112 - 113
  Torta di ciliege, 115
Dolce di caffè, 117

Eggplant Steaks, 96

Egg-White Frittata, 21

Fagioli ed orzo, 57
Fagioli stufati, 98 - 99
First Courses, 28 - 64
  Bean-Barley Soup, 57
  Cacciucco con battuto alla livornese,
    58 - 59
  Fagioli ed orzo, 57
  Fish Soup with Chopped Vegetables
    Livorno-Style, 58 - 59
  Grandmother's Kerchiefs (Stuffed
    Pasta Squares), 47 - 49
  Green Lasagne Naples-Style, 38 - 39
  Lasagne verdi alla napoletana, 38 - 39
  Macaroni Cooked in an Herbed
    Vegetable Sauce, 62
  Minestrone alla genovese, 54 - 55
  Minestrone Genoese-Style with Pesto
    Sauce, 54 - 55
  Orecchiette con cavolfiore, 42 - 43
  Orecchiette with Cauliflower, 42 - 43
  Parsley Pasta in Majoram Cream
    Sauce, 34 - 35
  Pasta al brodetto, 60 - 61
  Pasta alle erbe alla napoletana, 62
  Pasta allo zafferano, 32 - 33
  Pasta alle zucchine con gamberi, 50 - 51
  Pasta with Savory Uncooked
    Vegetable Sauce, 56
  Pasta with Scallops in Fish Sauce, 60 - 61
  Pasta with Zucchini and Shrimp, 50 - 51
  Peas and Paternostri, 52 - 53
  Pezze della nonna, 47 - 49
  Piselli e paternostri, 52 - 53
  Polenta con mascarpone e tartufi, 46 - 47
  Polenta with Mascarpone and White
    Truffles, 46 - 47
  Quadrucci alla maggiorana, 34 - 35
  Risotto ai peperoni, 63
  Risotto alla milanese, 44 - 45
  Risotto Milan-Style, 44 - 45
  Risotto with Sweet Bell Peppers, 63
  Saffron Pasta, 32 - 33
  Sedanini alla crudaiola in salsa piccante, 56
  Spaghetti alla Sangiovannino, 40 - 41

Spaghetti al sugo di cavolfiore, 64
Spaghetti with Air-Dried Cherry
    Tomatoes, 40 - 41
Spaghetti with Cauliflower Sauce, 64
Tagliatelle con dadi di prosciutto, 30 - 31
Tagliatelle with Creamed Prosciutto
    Sauce, 30 - 31
Tortelli alla parmigiana o di erbette,
    36 - 37
Tortelli Parma-Style, 36 - 37
Fish Soup with Chopped Vegetables
    Livorno-Style, 58 - 59
Focaccia al basilico, 70 - 71
Focaccia di patate, 100 - 101
Focaccia with Basil, 70 - 71
Frittata di bianchi, 21
Frutta in padella con salsa alla vaniglia,
    120 - 121

Grains and Pulses, 14 - 15, 44 - 46, 63
    Bean Paste Canapés, 14 - 15
    Crostini di fagioli, 14 - 15
    Polenta con mascarpone e tartufi, 46
    Polenta with Mascarpone and White
        Truffles, 46
    Risotto ai peperoni, 63
    Risotto alla milanese, 44 - 45
    Risotto Milan-Style, 44 - 45
    Risotto with Sweet Bell Peppers, 63
Grandmother's Kerchiefs (Stuffed Pasta
    Squares), 47 - 49
Green Lasagne Naples-Style, 38 - 39
Grissini al ramerino, 72 - 73

Insalata di cappone, 18 - 19
Insalata di peperoni e capperi , 10 - 11
Involtini di pesce spada, 78 - 79

Lamb with Herbed Horseradish Sauce, 94
Lasagne verdi alla napoletana, 38 - 39
Lemon Timbales, 118 - 119
Limoni in forma, 118 - 119
"Lift Me Up," 111
Liquore al mandarino, 106 - 107

Macaroni Cooked in an Herbed
    Vegetable Sauce, 62

Main Courses, 74 - 94
    Agnello alle erbe, 94
    Canestrelli di Chioggia, 80
    Carpaccio, 81
    Chicken Baked with Peppers, 87
    Chicken and Veal Galantine-Sausage
        with Green Peppercorns, 84 - 85
    Chicken Roasted with Lemon Halves, 86
    Cornmeal-Buckwheat Polenta with
        Pork Stew, 92 - 93
    Involtini di pesce spada, 78 - 79
    Lamb with Herbed Horseradish Sauce, 94
    Marinated Fried Sole Venetian-Style,
        76 - 77
    Ossobuco alle verdure, 82 - 83
    Ossobuco in a Vegetable Sauce, 82 - 83
    Pollo ai limoni, 86
    Pollo ai peperoni al forno, 87
    *Polenta taragna con spezzatino di
        maiale*, 92 - 93
    Roasted Veal Shank, 88 - 89
    Rolled Stuffed Swordfish Cutlets on
        Skewers, 78 - 79
    Salsiccia di pollo e vitella al pepe verde,
        84 - 85
    Scallops Chioggia-Style, 80
    Shrimp on Skewers with Thyme
        Sauce, 90 - 91
    Sogliole in saor, 76 - 77
    Spiedini di gamberi in salsa, 90 - 91
    Stracotto di vitella alla fornarina, 88 - 89
Marinated Capon Breast, 18 - 19
Marinated Fried Sole Venetian-Style, 76 - 77
Marsala Tart with Strawberries, 112 - 113
Marinated Whole Peaches with Mint, 116
Meats, 81 - 83, 88 - 89, 92 - 94
    Agnello alle erbe, 94
    Carpaccio, 81
    Cornmeal-Buckwheat Polenta with
        Pork Stew, 92 - 93
    Lamb with Herbed Horseradish Sauce, 94
    Ossobuco alle verdure, 82 - 83
    Ossobuco in a Vegetable Sauce, 82 - 83
    *Polenta taragna con spezzatino di
        maiale*, 92 - 93
    Roasted Veal Shank, 88 - 89
    Stracotto di vitella alla fornarina, 88 - 89

Minestrone alla genovese, 54 - 55
Minestrone Genoese-Style with Pesto
    Sauce, 54 - 55
Mozzarella Grilled on Skewers Roman-
    Style, 20

Orange Liqueur, 106 - 107
Orecchiette con cavolfiore, 42 - 43
Orecchiette with Cauliflower, 42 - 43
Ossobuco alle verdure, 82 - 83
Ossobuco in a Vegetable Sauce, 82 - 83

Pane di prato, 66 - 67
Panna cotta, 110
Panzanella del Valdarno, 22 - 23
Parsley Pasta in Majoram Cream Sauce, 34 - 35
Pasta, 30 - 43, 47 - 53, 56, 60 - 62, 64
    Grandmother's Kerchiefs (Stuffed
        Pasta Squares), 47 - 49
    Green Lasagne Naples-Style, 38 - 39
    Lasagne verdi alla napoletana, 38 - 39
    Macaroni Cooked in an Herbed
        Vegetable Sauce, 62
    Orecchiette con cavolfiore, 42 - 43
    Orecchiette with Cauliflower, 42 - 43
    Parsley Pasta in Majoram Cream
        Sauce, 35
    Pasta al brodetto, 60 - 61
    Pasta alle erbe alla napoletana, 62
    Pasta alle zucchine con gamberi, 50 - 51
    Pasta allo zafferano, 32 - 33
    Pasta with Savory Uncooked
        Vegetable Sauce, 56
    Pasta with Scallops in Fish Sauce, 60 - 61
    Pasta with Zucchini and Shrimp, 50 - 51
    Peas and Paternostri, 52 - 53
    Pezze della nonna, 47 - 49
    Piselli e paternostri, 52 - 53
    Quadrucci alla maggiorana, 35
    Saffron Pasta, 32 - 33
    Sedanini alla crudaiola in salsa piccante, 56
    Spaghetti alla Sangiovannino, 40 - 41
    Spaghetti al sugo di cavolfiore, 64
    Spaghetti with Air-Dried Cherry
        Tomatoes, 40 - 41
    Spaghetti with Cauliflower Sauce, 64
    Tagliatelle con dadi di prosciutto, 30 - 31

Tagliatelle with Creamed Prosciutto Sauce, 30 - 31
Tortelli alla parmigiana o di erbette, 36 - 37
Tortelli Parma-Style, 36 - 37
Pasta al brodetto, 60 - 61
Pasta alle erbe alla napoletana, 62
Pasta allo zafferano, 32 - 33
Pasta with Savory Uncooked Vegetable Sauce, 56
Pasta with Scallops in Fish Sauce, 60 - 61
Pasta alle zucchine con gamberi, 50 - 51
Pasta with Zucchini and Shrimp, 50 - 51
Patate con finocchio, 102 - 103
Pears Stuffed with Cream and Chocolate, 108 - 109
Peas and Paternostri, 52 - 53
Peperonata all'arrabbiata, 104
Pepper Salad with Capers, 10 - 11
Pere ripiene al cioccolato, 108 - 109
Pesche alla menta, 116
Pezze della nonna, 47 - 49
Piselli e paternostri, 52 - 53
Polenta con mascarpone e tartufi, 46
Polenta with Mascarpone and White Truffles, 46
Polenta taragna con spezzatino di maiale, 92 - 93
Pollo ai limoni, 86
Pollo ai peperoni al forno, 87
Poultry, 18 - 19, 84 - 87
    Chicken Baked with Peppers, 87
    Chicken and Veal Galantine-Sausage with Green Peppercorns, 84 - 85
    Chicken Roasted with Lemon Halves, 86
    Insalata di cappone, 18 - 19
    Marinated Capon Breast, 18 - 19
    Pollo ai limoni, 86
    Pollo ai peperoni al forno, 87
    Salsiccia di pollo e vitella al pepe verde, 84 - 85
Potatoes with Fennel, 102 - 103
Pulses and Grains, see Grains and Pulses

Quadrucci alla maggiorana, 34 - 35

Risotto ai peperoni, 63
Risotto alla milanese, 44 - 45

Risotto Milan-Style, 44 - 45
Risotto with Sweet Bell Peppers, 63
Roasted Veal Shank, 88 - 89
Rolled Stuffed Swordfish Cutlets on Skewers, 78 - 79
Rosemary Grissini, 72 - 73

Saffron Pasta, 32 - 33
Sage Batter Cake, 26 - 27
Salads, 10 - 11, 22 - 23
    Bread Salad, 22 - 23
    Insalata di peperoni e capperi, 10 - 11
    Panzanella del Valdarno, 22 - 23
    Pepper Salad with Capers, 10 - 11
Salsiccia di pollo e vitella al pepe verde, 84 - 85
Salviata, 26 - 27
Sautéed Fruit with Vanilla Sauce, 120 - 121
Scallops Chioggia-Style, 80
Schiacciata con uva, 68 - 69
Schiacciata with Fresh Grapes, 68 - 69
Seafood, 50 - 51, 58 - 61, 76 - 80, 90 - 91
    Cacciucco con battuto alla livornese, 58 - 59
    Canestrelli di Chioggia, 80
    Fish Soup with Chopped Vegetables Livorno-Style, 58 - 59
    Involtini di pesce spada, 78 - 79
    Marinated Fried Sole Venetian-Style, 76 - 77
    Pasta al brodetto, 60 - 61
    Pasta alle zucchine con gamberi, 50 - 51
    Pasta with Scallops in Fish Sauce, 60 - 61
    Pasta with Zucchini and Shrimp, 50 - 51
    Rolled Stuffed Swordfish Cutlets on Skewers, 78 - 79
    Scallops Chioggia-Style, 80
    Shrimp on Skewers with Thyme Sauce, 90 - 91
    Sogliole in saor, 76 - 77
    Spiedini di gamberi in salsa, 90 - 91
Sedanini alla crudaiola in salsa piccante, 56
Shrimp on Skewers with Thyme Sauce, 90 - 91
Sogliole in saor, 76 - 77
Soups, 54 - 55, 57
    Bean-Barley Soup, 57
    Fagioli ed orzo, 57
    Minestrone alla genovese, 54 - 55

Minestrone Genoese-Style with Pesto Sauce, 54 - 55
Spaghetti alla Sangiovannino, 40 - 41
Spaghetti al sugo di cavolfiore, 64
Spaghetti with Air-Dried Cherry Tomatoes, 40 - 41
Spaghetti with Cauliflower Sauce, 64
Spicy Peperonata, 104
Spiedini alla romano, 20
Spiedini di gamberi in salsa, 90 - 91
Stracotto di vitella alla fornarina, 88 - 89
Stuffed Potato Focaccia, 100 - 101

Tagliatelle con dadi di prosciutto, 30 - 31
Tagliatelle with Creamed Prosciutto Sauce, 30 - 31
Tomato Tart, 24 - 25
Torta al marsala con fragole, 112 - 113
Torta di ciliege, 115
Torta di funghi, 12 - 13
Torta di pomodoro, 24 - 25
Tortelli alla parmigiana o di erbette, 36 - 37
Tortelli Parma-Style, 36 - 37
Tiramisù, 111
Tuscan Beans Baked with Tuna and Lemon, 98 - 99

Vegetables, 12 - 13, 24 - 25, 95 - 104
    Artichokes with Peas Roman-Style, 97
    Bistecche di melanzane, 96
    Carciofi e piselli alla romana, 97
    Eggplant Steaks, 96
    Fagioli stufati, 98 - 99
    Focaccia di patate, 100 - 101
    Patate con finocchio, 102 - 103
    Peperonata all'arrabbiata, 104
    Potatoes with Fennel, 102 - 103
    Spicy Peperonata, 104
    Stuffed Potato Focaccia, 100 - 101
    Tomato Tart, 24 - 25
    Torta di funghi, 12 - 13
    Torta di pomodoro, 24 - 25
    Tuscan Beans Baked with Tuna and Lemon, 98 - 99
    Wild Mushroom Tart, 12 - 13

Wild Mushroom Tart, 12 - 13